One Giant Leap

THE GIANTS' REMARKABLE RUN TO THE NFL CHAMPIONSHIP

Star-Ledger nj.com

Everything Jersey

Published by Pediment Publishing, a division of The Pediment Group, Inc. www.pediment.com Printed in Canada

CONTENTS

LEFT: Michael Strahan and Eli Manning celebrate the team's victory during the ticker tape parade as they ride up the "Canyon of Heroes" on their way to city hall in Manhattan.
Photo by Andrew Mills

Foreword

I have covered all 42 Super Bowls and I never saw anything even remotely resembling what happened on Feb. 3, 2008, during a magical night in Glendale, Arizona.

I never saw anything like the way Eli Manning, squeezed by a two-headed 519-pound New England Patriots' "blitz monster" escaped to throw the pass that was seen and felt and almost heard all through the Great Megalopolis.

I never saw anything remotely resembling the catch David Tyree seemed to make off the top of his helmet almost as though he had a third hand.

And I never saw anything quite like the way he brought that ball in with him as he fell but managed to keep "the dream" alive.

I never saw anything like the way the Giants' down linemen played defense with the ferocity of a pack of starving wolves.

Hell, the simple truth is I never saw anything even resembling the way the Giants got to this postseason tournament in the first place after taking horrendous beatings in their first two games.

Somebody should write a book about this.

Forget somebody. You are about to enter the world of a lot of somebodys. Scratch that. Instead, make it the best damned group of somebodys ever to cover a season of football that was as much popcorn, toy balloons and real life fairy tales as it was a belly-to-belly and nose-to-nose Giants season to end all football seasons.

Inside these pages you will find the greening of Eli Manning, kid brother to a superstar, maligned young quarterback to Super Bowl MVP.

You will find the bruised leg and flourishing courage of Plaxico Burress, who caught the touchdown pass that produced the storybook ending.

You will find a group of ferocious down linemen and linebackers who took down the Patriots and cut short Bill Belichick's run at the NFL history book.

You will find the saga of Lawrence Tynes, the kicker thrice blessed with a shot at destiny and who, on his third try, launched the kick into the frigid night, the kick that sent the Giants from Green Bay to Super Bowl XLII.

It's all here, the coach who made it happen and the cast of players who refused to lose. It's here through the skill and the brilliance of a staff of terrific writers who were there and the camera's eye of the best group of photographers in the state.

So turn the page and enter the damnedest 100-yard wonderland there ever was.

Enjoy. It was a once in a lifetime year.

— *Jerry Izenberg*

LEFT: Plaxico Burress celebrates winning the Super Bowl with his son.
Photo by Chris Faytok

MAKING A STAND
THE FIRST HALF OF THE SEASON

By Mike Garafolo

A season of improbable events — a metamorphosis of a coach and a quarterback, a stunning streak of road victories, a didn't-see-that-coming playoff run that led to an appearance in Super Bowl XLII — really began with a simple football play.

A few of them in fact.

The Redskins were lined up at the 1-yard line in the closing seconds of a week three game in Washington, trailing by a touchdown. A score — and a possible 0-3 start for the Giants — appeared imminent.

It was then that the Giants' defense — one that had given up 80 points in season-opening losses to Dallas and Green Bay, one that The Star-Ledger had dubbed the worst unit in team history — made a stand.

Second down. Incompletion.

Third down. Goal-line stuff.

Fourth down. A season-saving tackle.

It was victory. And vindication.

"At that point, it's not about technique, it's not about the call, it's all about getting fired up and realizing what's at stake,"

defensive tackle Barry Cofield said. "We just came off the ball and did what we had to do."

These plays set the stage for the rest of the first half of the season. It was the first of six consecutive victories.

There was a 16-3 victory over the Eagles the following week on Monday Night Football when the defense tied an NFL record with 12 sacks, including six by Osi Umenyiora, and produced a touchdown when Kawika Mitchell returned a fumble 17 yards for a score. That win moved the Giants to .500 at 2-2.

Then there was a 35-24 victory over the Jets — a victory that showed one area team was up while the other was down. This time the offense got in the act as Plaxico Burress turned a short pass into a 53-yard touchdown for the go-ahead score in the fourth quarter.

A 31-10 dismantling of the Falcons in Atlanta on Monday Night Football when Eli Manning threw for 303 yards and two touchdowns came next.

The Giants were on a roll at 4-2. Overconfident? Not this bunch. This team remembered how it started.

"Honestly, I think the reason we're playing so good is because we've still got that

0-2 mentality," middle linebacker Antonio Pierce said after the Falcons game. "We went into this game thinking we were the 1-4 team."

Next up was a 33-15 rout of the 49ers — followed by another wake-up call, on another continent.

A game against the 0-7 Dolphins at Wembley Stadium in London was anything but easy. The Giants learned they couldn't take anything for granted, winning in an ugly rain game that was all drizzle and no sizzle, 13-10.

Still, the now 6-2 Giants had plenty to be thankful for.

The offense was clicking behind Manning and Burress, who hooked up for eight touchdowns in the first eight games. The defense — the one that yielded 80 points in the first two games — gave up just 79 in the next six.

This team earned its bye week.

"It's been a hard three weeks — a Monday night (game against the Falcons), then come back for an early Sunday game (vs. the 49ers), and then fly over here and play with a five-hour time difference," defensive end Michael Strahan said after the victory over the Dolphins. "I think everybody responded well. It just shows we're going to stick together." ■

LEFT: Giants quarterback Eli Manning just avoids getting sacked by the Jets' Shaun Ellis early in the first quarter in week five. *Photo by Tony Kurdzuk*

Game 1: Doomsday in Dallas
Cowboys 45, Giants 35
Texas Stadium
Irving, Texas

A Texas shootout? More like a blowout.

Eli Manning threw for 312 yards and four touchdowns and Plaxico Burress had eight catches for 144 yards and three touchdowns. But don't be fooled, there was no reason for joy after this one.

A few things became clear: Eli Manning wasn't the best quarterback on the field (that honor went to the Cowboys' Tony Romo) and the Giants weren't the best team. Not by a long shot.

After yielding 45 points — and recording just one sack — defensive end Michael Strahan summed up the defense. And the Giants as a whole.

"We have a lot of work to do," he said. "This was indicative of that."

The back-and-forth game turned in the third quarter. Down 24-19 and needing a score, Manning and the offense produced a three-and-out.

Romo and the Cowboys were ready. After getting the ball back on their own 33, they needed just four plays to extend their lead to 31-19 on a 9-yard scramble by Romo around

RIGHT: The Giants' Jeremy Shockey can't hold onto a pass as the Packers' Tramon Williams defends. *Photo by Tim Farrell*

OPPOSITE: Giants defense gang takles the Packers' DeShawn Wynn. *Photo by Tim Farrell*

linebacker Mathias Kiwanuka.

The Giants tried to answer, but their ensuing drive was halted at the 6 and produced just a Lawrence Tynes field goal, trimming the lead to nine in the opening minutes of the fourth quarter. That's when Romo and Terrell Owens delivered the knockout punch — a 47-yard touchdown on a crossing route for a 38-22 lead.

A few late scores padded some offensive stats but did nothing to close a seemingly large gap between the Cowboys and Giants.

— *Mike Garafolo*

Week 2: Woe-and-Two
Packers 35, Giants 13
Giants Stadium
East Rutherford, NJ

The first blowout loss you could chalk up to a fluke, but the second set off alarm bells.

By the time a rejuvenated Brett Favre was done shredding the defense for 286 yards and three touchdowns, the Giants had given up 80 points in the first two games of the season — the most through two games since giving up a franchise-record 86 in the first two weeks of the 1966 season.

Even worse, they were 0-2 for the first time since 1996.

"I do believe we're all in it together," coach Tom Coughlin said, "and I do believe we're all embarrassed."

Eli Manning shook off a shoulder injury, suffered in the opener, to complete 16 of 29 passes for 211 yards, a touchdown, and an interception, but the real story was the wretched Giants defense, particularly the secondary. Favre was 11-for-11 in the third quarter alone.

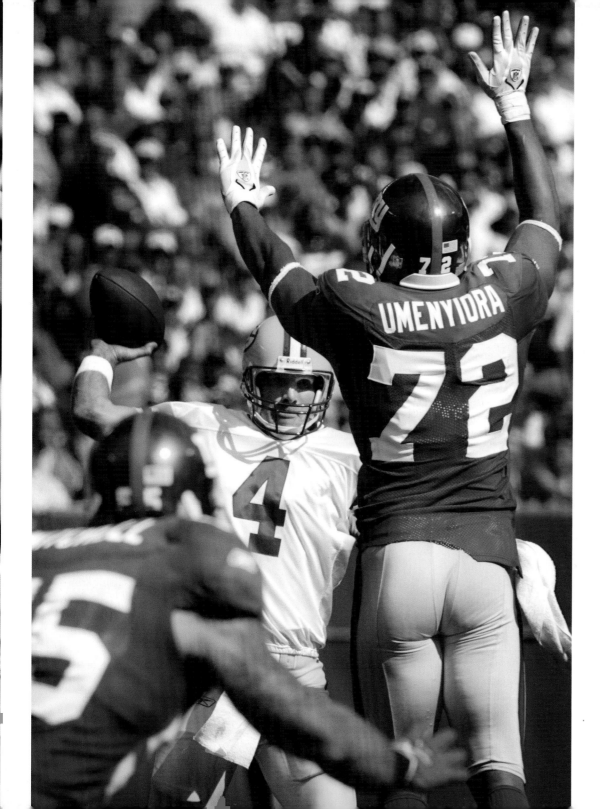

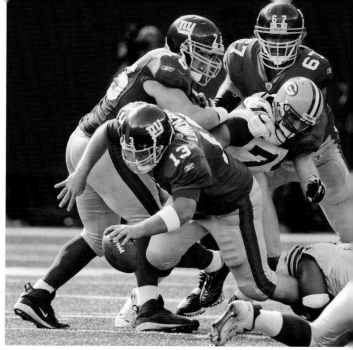

ABOVE: Giants backup quarterback Jared Lorenzen is sacked in the second half. *Photo by Tim Farrell*

LEFT: Packers quarterback Brett Favre throws a pass over the out-stretched arms of Giants defensive end Osi Umenyiora. *Photo by Joe Epstein*

OPPOSITE: Derrick Ward flies through the air after a tackled by the Packers' Nick Collins. *Photo by Tim Farrell*

"It could have been any quarterback," Giants corner Sam Madison said. "... But when you have a Hall of Fame quarterback like that who can see everything, can see the field, knows where people are going to be, knows what they're going to do and knows his offense the way he does (makes it) extremely hard."

In addition, two costly Giants' penalties turned potential touchdown drives into field goals in the ugly loss, leaving the team staring at some unwelcome statistics: from 1990 to 2006, only 18 of 139 teams that started 0-2 made the playoffs.

— *Mike Garafolo*

OPPOSITE: Giants quarterback Eli Manning tackles the Packers' Corey Williams after Williams intercepted a Manning pass. *Photo by Tim Farrell*

LEFT: Antonio Pierce reflects as the final seconds of the game tick off. *Photo by Tim Farrell*

Week 3: The Big Stop
Giants 24, Redskins 17
FedEx Field
Landover, Md.

One yard stood between a Giants win and another embarrassment. Only the beleaguered Giants defense stood in between.

But improbably, a unit which had given up 846 yards in the first two games defended all 36 inches of the last one. Three stops on a last-minute goal-line stand allowed a fourth-quarter touchdown pass from Eli Manning to Plaxico Burress to stand up and gave the Giants a victory over the Redskins that kept them from falling three games behind Washington in the NFC East.

"It's not good to be 0-2 in this league," said defensive end Michael Strahan, who was celebrating all alone near midfield after end Justin Tuck and rookie corner Aaron Ross tackled Ladell Betts in the backfield on fourth-and-goal to seal the win. "And to come here and to have a game that tight ... for us to stop them like that, it was a lot of emotion, a lot of relief just for this team.

"And I think this should be a confidence builder for us with the defense and the team as a whole."

In all the jubilant post-game celebration, it was almost hard to remember that the Giants trailed the Redskins 17-3 at halftime, looking well on their way to another mortifying loss.

But then the defense clamped down and the offense turned it on, outscoring the Redskins 14-0 in the pivotal fourth quarter, setting up the defense's definitive goal-line stand.

— *Mike Garafolo*

LEFT: Michael Strahan relaxes during pregame warmups at FedEx Field. *Photo by Andrew Mills*

RIGHT: Giants wide receiver Plaxico Burress runs for the end zone for a touchdown to put the Giants ahead in the fourth quarter.
Photo by Andrew Mills

OPPOSITE: Eli Manning puts his arms up to signal a touchdown as the Giants' Reuben Droughns scores his second touchdown of the game.
Photo by Andrew Mills

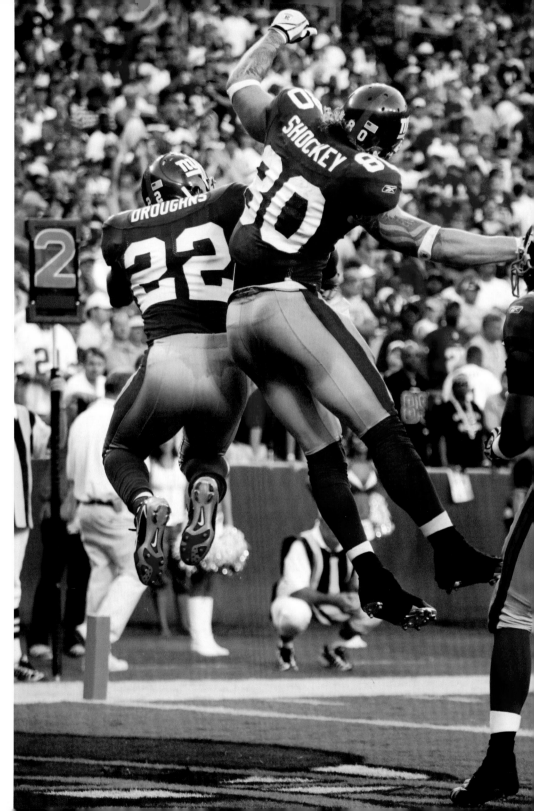

ABOVE: Eli Manning scrambles out of trouble against the
Washington Redskins. *Photo by Andrew Mills*

RIGHT: Giants Reuben Droughns and Jeremy Shockey celebrate
Droughns' second touchdown of the game. *Photo by Andrew Mills*

OPPOSITE: Giants tight end Jeremy Shockey smiles after making a
21-yard catch at the Redskins' 1-yard line. Making the tackle for the
Skins was LaRon Landry and Rocky McIntosh. *Photo by Andrew Mills*

Week 4: The "Sack Pack"
Giants 16, Eagles 3
Giants Stadium
East Rutherford, NJ

Donovan McNabb is still sore from this one.

The Giants tied an NFL record by sacking the Eagles quarterback 12 times, evening their record at 2-2 and pushing the defense's struggles of the first two games further into the past.

Right defensive end Osi Umenyiora set a single-game team record with six sacks while left end Michael Strahan had his first of the season, giving him 133.5 for his career and making him the franchise's new all-time sack king.

Mathias Kiwanuka had three sacks and Justin Tuck added two, giving the Giants four pass-rushing ends all of the team's sacks.

"Everybody was just (saying), `It's like a video game when we go out there,'" said Umenyiora.

The effort was masterminded by defensive coordinator Steve Spagnuolo, who spent his last eight years in Philadelphia as a defensive assistant before being hired by the Giants in the offseason. His defense stretched a scoreless streak to 77 minutes, nine seconds

OPPOSITE: The Giants' Kawika Mitchell runs back an Eagles fumble for a touchdown in the second half.
Photo by Tim Farrell

LEFT: Another sack for Osi Umenyiora, this time causing Donovan McNabb to fumble in the fourth quarter.
Photo by Tim Farrell

ABOVE: Giants defensive end Michael Strahan celebrates his sack during the second quarter. That sack gave Strahan the Giants' all-time career sack record. *Photo by Andrew Mills*

RIGHT: Jeremy Shockey is brought down by the Jets' Eric Smith. *Photo by Tony Kurdzuk*

before the Eagles kicked a field goal in the fourth quarter.

The defense also contributed to the offense, as linebacker Kawika Mitchell returned a fumble by McNabb 17 yards for a touchdown in the third quarter. That put the Giants ahead, 16-0, thanks to a second-quarter touchdown pass from Eli Manning (14-for-26 for 135 yards) to Plaxico Burress and a field goal by Lawrence Tynes, who also missed an extra point.

— *Mike Garafolo*

Week 5: Jeers to Cheers
Giants 35, Jets 24
Giants Stadium
East Rutherford, NJ

It was a Giants home game, so it made sense the fans in blue would be louder than those in green.

At halftime, they were. Only they weren't cheering. They were booing a few of the coaches' decisions — benching the promising rookie, calling for passes instead of runs and trying for a late second-quarter score instead of limiting further damage.

A half-hour of football later, they were cheering coach Tom Coughlin's 100th career victory. The Giants, in an increasingly familiar pattern, had survived to beat the Jets, thanks to wide receiver Plaxico Burress' 53-yard touchdown in the fourth quarter .

As for the benched rookie, cornerback Aaron Ross? His interception preceded Bur-

LEFT: Giants guard Chris Snee and Jets defensive tackle Dewayne Robertson collide during the first quarter.
Photo by Tony Kurdzuk

23

ress' score, and he iced the game by returning his second interception 43 yards for a touchdown with 3:15 to play.

"Resilient," said defensive end Justin Tuck, who had five tackles. "That's a good word. That's exactly what we are. And I'm telling you, we don't even hear the boos."

The Giants trailed 17-7 at the half, after an anemic first two quarters that resulted in just 75 yards rushing and 22 yards passing. But when the Jets sputtered in the second half, the Giants were able to take advantage, capping the rally with Burress' touchdown sprint down the left sideline, his seventh TD of the season.

"We were in the face of adversity in the early part of the (season)," linebacker Kawika Mitchell said. "And today we faced it earlier in the game. It was just a test of how we were going to handle it."

— *Mike Garafolo*

Week 6: Putting it Together
Giants 31, Falcons 10
The Georgia Dome
Atlanta

No last-minute heroics were needed this time.

The 1-5 Falcons played like their record, while the Giants played like the team on the upswing in their most complete game of the season.

They threw the ball, they ran it, they rushed the quarterback, played good pass defense and even got solid play on special teams. Plus, there were few mental errors and penalties to stall their own

OPPOSITE: Aaron Ross leaps over the goal line as he scores a touchdown after grabbing an interception in the fourth quarter. *Photo by Tony Kurdzuk*

LEFT: Giants running back Brandon Jacobs moves the ball in the fourth quarter against the Jets. *Photo by Tony Kurdzuk*

ABOVE: Giants receiver Plaxico Burress pushes off Jets defensive back Andre Dyson as he runs in for a touchdown in the fourh quarter.
Photo by Tony Kurdzuk

RIGHT: Plaxico Burress bows to the fans as he celebrates the touchdown that put the Giants ahead, 27-24. *Photo by Tony Kurdzuk*

drives, allowing the offense to gain a season-high 491 total yards.

Eli Manning completed 27 of 39 passes (including 12 straight at one point) for 303 yards and two touchdowns. He made two bad passes and both were intercepted.

But Manning's pair of mistakes didn't matter. Not with Plaxico Burress proving once again that practice is apparently overrated. He played impressively through a sprained ankle, catching six passes for 97 yards, including a 43-yard touchdown in the first half — his eighth of the season.

The running game chipped in as well, behind back Reuben Droughns, who scored his third touchdown of the season in addition to gaining 90 yards. Brandon Jacobs added 86 yards while Derrick Ward had 12 and a touchdown.

The win put the surging Giants only one game behind the Cowboys for first place in the NFC East.

— *Mike Garafolo*

LEFT: Defensive end Osi Umenyiora is tended to by medical personnel after being shaken up on a play in which he sacked Jets quarterback Chad Pennington. *Photo by Andrew Mills*

OPPOSITE: Giants head coach Tom Coughlin and Michael Strahan congratulate Aaron Ross after Ross made an interception and touchdown. *Photo by Tony Kurdzuk*

BELOW: The Giants' Sam Madison breaks up a pass intended for the Jets' Jerricho Cotchery. *Photo by Tony Kurdzuk*

ABOVE: Eli Manning shakes hands with Jets quarterback Chad Pennington after the Giants beat the Jets, 35-24. *Photo by Andrew Mills*

Week 7: Turnover Takedown
Giants 33, 49ers 15
Giants Stadium
East Rutherford, NJ

By week seven, no one in the NFL was having as much fun — or wreaking as much havoc — as the Giants' defense.

The unit, anchored by a devastating pass rush, had six sacks, two interceptions and two fumble recoveries in their fifth consecutive victory.

"They can't come up with new schemes to block us all, you understand?" defensive end Osi Umenyiora said.

The offense turned the four turnovers into 24 points — seven of which were the result of a sack, forced fumble, recovery and touchdown return by Umenyiora in the third quarter that linebacker Kawika Mitchell called "the ultimate play." Umenyiora swiped the ball from 49ers quarterback Trent Dilfer, grabbed the ball on one bounce and showed his speed for 75 yards to the end zone.

The Giants won despite five dropped passes, four penalties on special teams, a missed extra point and a blocked punt. That's because the pass rush compensated for everything else. The Giants, who entered the game with a league-high 21 sacks, added

LEFT: Giants defensive end Justin Tuck is held by 49ers offensive tackle Jonas Jennings as he rushes quarterback Trent Dilfer. *Photo by Tim Farrell*

six more and a whole lot more pressure on Dilfer.

The only thing casting a shadow on the streaking Giants was the fact that in their five-game run they had beaten only one team with a winning record (the 4-2 Redskins).

But as the team rolled to another win, no one wanted to spoil the positive vibe.

"I've been saying this since training camp: This is the tightest-knit chemistry group that we've had, and I think that's what you see every Sunday," linebacker Antonio Pierce said. "When things go bad, the offense messes up, the defense tries to go out there and make a play. When the defense makes a mistake, the offense tries to recover."

— *Mike Garafolo*

Week 8: London Calling
Giants 13, Dolphins 10
Wembley Stadium
London, England

The scene was gimmicky and the fans didn't really grasp the concept. The weather was awful and the field conditions worse.

The take-home point for the Giants, though, remained the same — another win. That pushed them to 6-2 on the season, within a half-game of the Cowboys for first place in the NFC East and set up a showdown with Dallas after their bye week.

The Giants kept the Dolphins winless

RIGHT: After forcing 49ers quarterback Trent Dilfer into a fumble, Osi Umenyiora scoops up the ball and runs it back for a touchdown. *Photo by Tim Farrell*

OPPOSITE: Umenyiora rumbles toward the end zone after recovering the Dilfer fumble. *Photo by Tim Farrell*

even though neither team was able to put much together in Wembley's muck. They combined for 14 penalties, three fumbles lost, two missed field goals and plenty of dropped passes.

Eli Manning ended up doing more with his legs than with his arm, adding a 10-yard touchdown run.

"When it was raining hard, the ball was slick," said Manning, who completed only 8 of 22 passes for 59 yards and a 44.9 passer rating.

Running back Brandon Jacobs had a career-high 131 yards on 23 carries, and the Giants survived a late rally by the Dolphins to go into their bye week on a six-game winning streak, exhausted but exultant.

— *Mike Garafolo*

LEFT: Osi Umenyiora raises the ball in triumph as he nears the end zone after recovering a Trent Dilfer fumble in the third quarter. *Photo by Tim Farrell*

HIGHS AND LOWS
SECOND HALF OF THE SEASON

By Mike Garafolo

There was renewed confidence because of their six-game winning streak. And renewed energy because of their week off.

When the Giants began the second half of their season with a home game against the Cowboys, they had every reason to believe they were ready to make a statement: Prove they could win games against the best teams in the conference.

But after a 31-20 loss that wasn't that close, the only statement they made was that they weren't ready for the big boys.

Confidence was replaced by questions: Would this now 6-3 team collapse down the stretch as the two previous teams had?

Energy was replaced by angst: If you can't

LEFT: The Giants' Plaxico Burress makes a stutter step move on Eagles safety Brian Dawkins for a 31-yard reception in the second half as the Eagles fall to the Giants, 16-13. *Photo by Andrew Mills*

stick with a good team at home, what would the rest of the season bring?

They found out the next week.

On the road against a much-improved Lions team, the Giants survived with a 16-10 victory. Then they took a step backward — make that two steps backward — with a 41-17 home loss to the Vikings in which Eli Manning threw four interceptions, three of which were returned for touchdowns.

"I wish there was some simple explanation for this game," Giants coach Tom Coughlin said, "but there isn't."

Looking back, there may have been.

The game was at Giants Stadium.

With their season on the line, the Giants went on a two-game road trip — rallying to beat the defending NFC champion Bears in Chicago, 21-16, then holding off the rival Eagles in Philadelphia, 16-13, when an Eagles' field-goal attempt hit the goal post in the final seconds.

A trend was developing as the now 9-4

Giants had won six in a row away from home.

A home game with the Redskins followed. And following the trend, the Giants looked awful in losing 22-10.

Then, with a playoff spot on the line and the Patriots looming in the final game, the Giants went on the road and clinched a spot in the postseason for a third straight season with a convincing 38-21 victory over the Bills. It was the team's seventh straight win away from home.

The biggest victory, however, may have come when head coach Tom Coughlin did not lose the locker room during an up-and-down season.

"There have been years here where the offense didn't like the defense and everybody was mad at the special teams. It was a mess," wide receiver Amani Toomer said. "When coach Coughlin came here, he calmed all of that down and we are trying to be more of a unit than we have in the past." ■

ABOVE: Giants tight end Jeremy Shockey sticks his tongue out after his touchdown reception in front of Cowboys safety Roy Williams. *Photo by Chris Faytok*

LEFT: Cowboys quarterback Tony Romo steps up in the pocket to elude the grasp of Michael Strahan and Justin Tuck just before throwing a touchdown pass to give the Cowboys a 7-0 lead. *Photo by Andrew Mills*

Week 10: Reality Check
Cowboys 31, Giants 20
Giants Stadium
East Rutherford, NJ

This was the Giants' chance at legitimacy. An opportunity to validate their six-game winning streak against inferior competition and pull into a tie for first place in the NFC East.

It was, as they themselves said, a "statement game."

But the only statement the Giants made in their loss to the Cowboys was that they were a lot closer to being the team that lost all three games against the NFC's elite than the one that padded its record against some of the worst teams in the NFL.

"I'm disappointed, there is no doubt about that," coach Tom Coughlin said during his postgame press conference, which he ended after only two questions by storming off the podium. "But I think we have a good football team and we will go back to work now."

Once again, Tony Romo out-dueled Eli Manning. The Giants' quarterback wasn't awful, going 23 of 34 passes for 236 yards, one

---

RIGHT: Giants defensive end Michael Strahan has words with Cowboys offensive tackle Marc Colombo. *Photo by Chris Faytok*

OPPOSITE: Cowboys wide receiver Terrell Owens scores on a 50-yard touchdown reception, beating Giants safety Gibril Wilson. *Photo by Chris Faytok*

ABOVE: Giants quarterback Eli Manning pulls off his hat as he prepares to go back out on the field late in the second half. *Photo by Andrew Mills*

RIGHT: Dallas WR Patrick Crayton shakes off Giants corner Aaron Ross for a touchdown late in the second quarter.

Photo by Andrew Mills

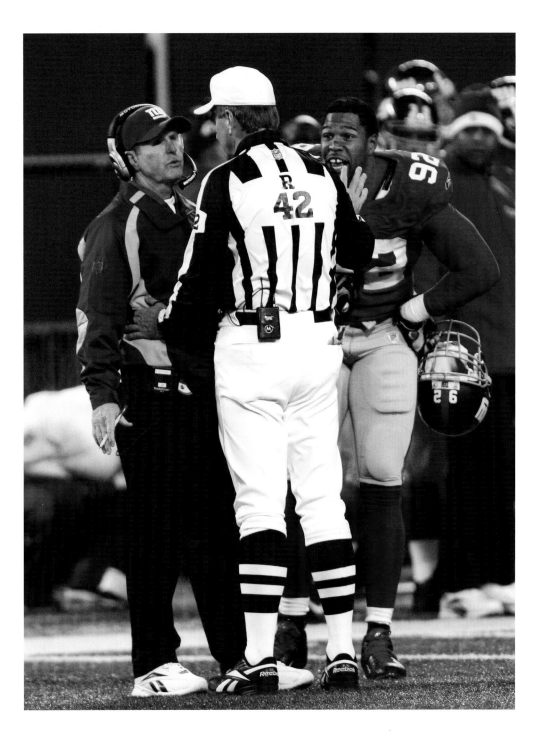

touchdown and two interceptions.

But Romo was better. The Cowboys' quarterback finished the game 20-for-28 for 247 yards, four touchdowns and one interception, finding wide receiver Terrell Owens six times for 125 yards and two touchdowns – the second of which was a game-clinching 50-yarder with 10:58 left.

"They hit a post ball into three-deep coverage," Coughlin said. "A long post for a touchdown which should have never happened into that coverage."

The loss dropped the Giants to 1-3 against teams with plus-.500 records, with their two losses against Dallas leaving them two games out of first place in the division with only seven weeks left in the season.

— *Mike Garafolo*

Week 11: Playoff Pursuit
Giants 16, Lions 10
Ford Field
Detroit

The Giants didn't spend much time lamenting their loss to Dallas.

One week later, they topped Detroit to keep their playoff hopes very much alive with a one-game lead and the tiebreaker over the Lions for the NFC's top wild-card spot.

"A lot of people didn't realize there were seven games left and guys were still hungry," said Sam Madison, who sealed the win with an interception on the Lions' final drive. "We wanted to prove something — and we did."

LEFT: Giants coach Tom Coughlin and defensive end Michael Strahan complain to Jeff Triplette late in the second half as the Giants fall to the Dallas Cowboys, 31-20.
Photo by Andrew Mills

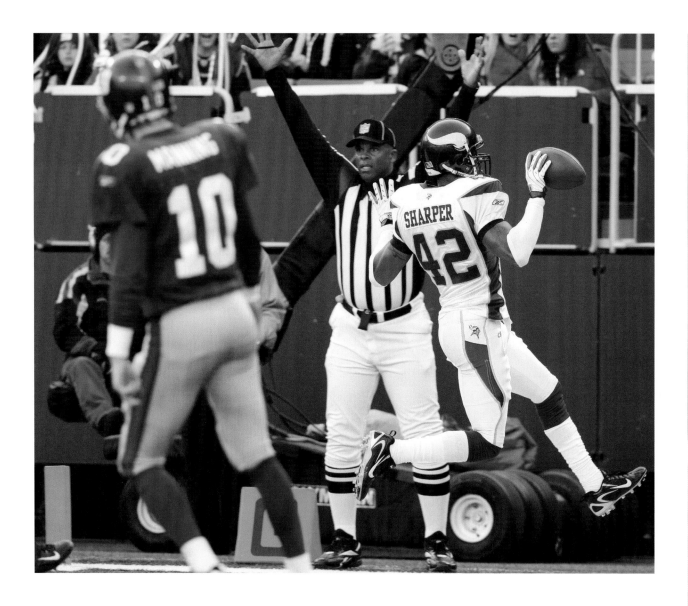

ABOVE: Giants quarterback Eli Manning looks on as Vikings safety Darren Sharper dances into the end zone with an interception. *Photo by Chris Faytok*

RIGHT: The Vikings' Charles Gordon knocks the ball away from Giants wide receiver Amani Toomer in the first half. *Photo by Tim Farrell*

The key to the game was the defense's four turnovers. They had three interceptions and recovered one fumble — all in Giants territory. The biggest of those takeaways was an interception by safety James Butler on a deep flag pattern by Shaun McDonald in the left side of the end zone with 1:54 left in the game and the Lions driving for a possible winning touchdown.

The Giants offense gained 341 yards and entered Lions territory six times, only to score one touchdown — a 10-yard catch-and-run by running back Brandon Jacobs.

Quarterback Eli Manning responded to yet another round of criticism after a game against the Cowboys that wasn't even one of his worst. Manning missed a few throws he should have completed, but he still connected on 28 of 39 passes for 283 yards. And he didn't throw an interception against a team that had 15 coming in.

"We felt we were going to have to come in and get a lot of points to win the game," Manning said. "The way it turned out, the defense was playing great."

— *Mike Garafolo*

Week 12: Eli Implodes
Vikings 41, Giants 17
Giants Stadium
East Rutherford, NJ

It was the kind of performance everyone thought — and hoped — that Eli Manning had left behind him.

But against the Vikings, the Giants' quarterback had one of his worst games of the season, raising questions about the legitimacy of the team's playoff chances.

After completing his first three passes,

45

ABOVE: The Vikings' Ben Leber downs Eli Manning on a fourth-down play in the fourth quarter. Manning lost 26 yards on the play. *Photo by Tim Farrell*

RIGHT: Giants defensive tackle Fred Robbins tries to get to Vikings quarterback Tarvaris Jackson as his helmet pops off during the first half. *Photo by Chris Faytok*

Manning connected on only three of his next 18, with big brother Peyton watching from a luxury box.

Three of Manning's four interceptions were returned for touchdowns — the first time in the NFL's past 23 seasons a team had at least that many. A Manning pass on third down late in the first quarter was picked off by Vikings safety Darren Sharper, who returned it 20 yards for a touchdown and a lead Minnesota never relinquished.

"Well, it wasn't good. When you throw four interceptions, it is never a good day," Manning said. "Every one has its own story."

Other problems — untimely penalties, a lack of a running game without Brandon Jacobs and Derrick Ward and more than a few missed tackles — plagued the Giants. But most of all, Manning was again unable to solve the Vikings, who entered the game with the NFL's worst pass defense but intercepted him a combined eight times in their last two meetings.

Even though at 7-4 the Giants maintained a one-game lead for the first NFC wild-card spot, the weak showing against the Vikings left them a dejected team seeking answers.

"We keep shooting ourselves in the foot," center Shaun O'Hara said. "We're running out of toes."

— *Mike Garafolo*

Week 13: Windy City Comeback
Giants 21, Bears 16
Soldier Field
Chicago

The Giants proved, once again, that you can never count them out.

Down 16-7 late in the fourth quarter, the Giants rallied past the Bears to improve to 8-4, two games ahead of the Lions, Cardinals and Vikings for the NFC's top wild-card spot.

"We came into this game looking to be 8-4," coach Tom Coughlin said, "and by the grace of God, we are 8-4."

After two straight weeks of struggles and ill-advised passes, Eli Manning somehow pulled it all together and went 7-for-9 for 95 yards on the Giants' final two drives, throwing a touchdown to Amani Toomer to cut the Bears' lead to two and then leading a game-winning drive that was capped by a 2-yard touchdown run by Reuben Droughns.

"You want a quarterback who's fearless, who's not afraid to make a mistake," Michael Strahan said. "All of us make mistakes. And for Eli to stand up, come back and do those things, hopefully that builds some confidence in him because, really, that's all this game is."

Toomer's touchdown catch, with 6:54

OPPOSITE: Giants quarterback Eli Manning on the sidelines during the fourth quarter after throwing his fourth interception of the game between the Giants and the Vikings at Giants Stadium. *Photo by Chris Faytok*

LEFT TOP: Giants head coach Tom Coughlin complains to a ref in the first half. *Photo by Tim Farrell*

LEFT BOTTOM: The Giants' Plaxico Burress looks up at the scoreboard in the fourth quarter. *Photo by Tim Farrell*

to play, was initially ruled incomplete, but he immediately ran toward the sideline and encouraged Coughlin to challenge the call.

It was overturned, and then the defense came up with a big stop. The banged-up unit, without cornerback Aaron Ross and safety Gibril Wilson, came up with a key three-and-out that was capped by the Giants' fifth sack of Grossman — this one split by end Justin Tuck and linebacker Kawika Mitchell.

— *Mike Garafolo*

Week 14: One Second Left
Giants 16, Eagles 13
Lincoln Financial Field
Philadelphia

This win came by inches.

Eagles' kicker David Akers' 57-yard field-goal attempt clanked off the right upright with one second left, giving the Giants the victory — bumping their record to 9-4 and moving them to the verge of clinching a playoff berth.

"Man, that goal post," Giants defensive end Michael Strahan said. "I'm glad it was right where it was."

Plaxico Burress had seven catches for 136 yards, including the game-winning 20-yard touchdown from Eli Manning, who was 17-of-31 and 219 yards in the game.

OPPOSITE: Plaxico Burress makes Eagles cornerback Sheldon Brown miss for a 31-yard reception in the second half of the Giants' game against the Philadelphia Eagles at Lincoln Financial Field. *Photo by Andrew Mills*

LEFT: Center Shaun O'Hara and the rest of the Giants' line prepare to do battle against the Eagles.
Photo by Andrew Mills

LEFT: Giants linebacker Antonio Pierce flattens Eagles wide receiver Jason Avant on a key fourth-down pass play late in the second half.
Photo by Andrew Mills

ABOVE: The Eagles' Juqua Thomas blocks a pass by Eli Manning.
Photo by Noah Addis

Manning stayed composed under pressure. After shaky performances against the Vikings and in the first three quarters against the Bears, Manning's strong finish in Chicago seemed to carry over. On one play in the second quarter, he slipped, had the awareness to protect the ball with two hands, calmly got back to his feet, looked for Burress and hit him for a key first down.

The Giants got the ball back late when Antonio Pierce hit wide receiver Jason Avant from behind as the ball arrived (or maybe a little before) on a fourth-and-6 from the Giants' 44-yard line with 2:19 to play.

The Giants then gained only 9 yards on three runs by running back Brandon Jacobs, forcing a punt from the Eagles' 47 with 1:03 to play.

Quarterback Donovan McNabb then drove the Eagles 50 yards in under one minute to set up the field-goal attempt.

"That made us the worst 9-4 team in the league," Jacobs said.

But when it hit off the upright, the Giants could celebrate another step closer to a playoff spot.

— *Mike Garafolo*

OPPOSITE: Osi Umenyiora sacks Donovan McNabb in the second quarter. *Photo by Noah Addis*

LEFT: Eagles kicker David Akers reacts after his potential game-tying kick hit the uprights with seconds remaining in the game. *Photo by Andrew Mills*

Week 15: A Tough Loss
Redskins 22, Giants 10
Giants Stadium
East Rutherford, NJ

Losing the game was bad enough. Losing Jeremy Shockey made the future look awfully bleak for the still-playoff-berth-less Giants.

The tight end fractured his left fibula in the third quarter when wide receiver Amani Toomer rolled onto his leg at the end of a 3-yard run by Brandon Jacobs. Shockey had surgery later that week and was forced to miss the rest of the season.

"That's a big loss," Jacobs said. "That's one on the jaw we have to take."

Even though a playoff berth remained in reach, there were plenty of concerns for the Giants after this one. In the frigid, gusty weather, Manning completed only 18 of 52 passes for 184 yards. He hurried a few throws, missed some open receivers and often threw nowhere near his intended target.

The offense overall managed only 110 total yards in the first half while converting only one of its first nine third downs and five of 19 overall.

OPPOSITE: The Giants' Steve Smith can't come up with this fourth-quarter pass as the Redskins' Reed Doughty defends on the play. No penalty was called despite protests by the Giants. *Photo by Tim Farrell*

LEFT: The Giants' Sinorice Moss misses the pass in the first half. *Photo by William Perlman*

The Giants finally got their act together in the third quarter on a six-play, 48-yard drive that Manning capped with a 19-yard touchdown pass to rookie tight end Kevin Boss — Shockey's replacement — that cut the Redskins' lead to 12.

But late in the third quarter, Toomer had an uncharacteristic drop, Manning missed an open Burress in the end zone and had a pass for Burress broken up by Redskins cornerback Fred Smoot. The drive ended with a missed 38-yard field-goal attempt by Lawrence Tynes.

The Giants could not convert on a last-gasp fourth-down play on their next possession, and that pretty much ended the game and the Giants' opportunity to clinch a playoff spot that day.

— *Mike Garafolo*

Week 16: Playoff Bound
Giants 38, Bills 21
Ralph Wilson Stadium
Orchard Park, N.Y.

It wasn't technically a must-win game, though it might as well have been. With a Week 17 matchup with the undefeated Patriots looming, this was the Giants' best chance to clinch a playoff berth.

In cold, wind, rain, and snow, they did just that, locking up a wild-card spot, the

OPPOSITE: Redskins quarterback Todd Collins scrambles as Justin Tuck closes in on him in the first half. *Photo by Tim Farrell*

LEFT: The Giants' Amani Toomer can't hold onto a pass in the end zone in the third quarter in a game against the Redskins. *Photo by Tim Farrell*

ABOVE: The Bills' Marshawn Lynch is tackled by Osi Umenyiora.
Photo by William Perlman

RIGHT: Eli Manning gets ready to take the snap as the rain came
down in the second quarter. *Photo by William Perlman*

ABOVE: Brandon Jacobs runs into the end zone for his second touchdown. *Photo by William Perlman*

OPPOSITE: The Giants' Zak DeOssie (51) and Craig Dahl (30) along with Reggie Torbor (53) celebrate in the fourth quarter. *Photo by William Perlman*

ABOVE: Kawika Mitchell and Michael Strahan get to the Bills' Trent Edwards in the fourth quarter. *Photo by William Perlman*

NFC's fifth seed and a date with the fourth-seeded Buccaneers in the first round of the playoffs.

"Merry Christmas," Antonio Pierce announced after helping to shower coach Tom Coughlin with celebratory Gatorade. "That was our Christmas present to him."

Brandon Jacobs rushed for 145 yards and two touchdowns on 24 carries, and rookie Ahmad Bradshaw ran for 151 yards on 17 attempts.

"I don't know what it was, but it was fun," right guard Chris Snee said. "Run after run after run after run. It really put it on us to get the job done. Those are opportunities that we love and we got the job done."

The Giants needed every yard to make up for the two interceptions and two fumbles lost by quarterback Eli Manning, who completed seven of 15 passes for 111 yards in another miserable cold-weather performance.

The teams traded leads amidst the awful conditions before Bradshaw put the game out of reach with an 88-yard touchdown run with 6:12 to play.

"We knew all week long it was going to be tight in there and they were going to play eight and nine guys in the box, because that's the way Buffalo's played all year long," Jacobs said. "I kind of knew (longer runs) were going to break at some point in time."

— *Mike Garafolo*

LEFT: Giants head coach Tom Coughlin gets doused after the Giants beat the Bills 38-21.
Photo by William Perlman

CLOSE TO PERFECT
WEEK 17: PATRIOTS 38, GIANTS 35

By Kevin Manahan

The Patriots: the team that has intimidated opponents, embarrassed mouthy opposing players and humiliated revered coaches by running up the score, completed the NFL's first 16-0 season. But they struggled to beat the Giants, 38-35, at Giants Stadium.

The Giants: the team with the sleepy-eyed quarterback. The unpredictable squad with the rigid, sometimes maniacal coach. The team with the tender-footed wide receiver and the tight end on crutches. The team with the hard-hitting running back with the even harder pass-catching hands.

The team with more broken legs than Refrigerator Perry's sofa gave the best team in the NFL all it could handle.

Eli Manning, the infuriatingly mild-mannered quarterback, threw four touchdown passes. The underdog Giants sacked

quarterback Tom Brady just once. When wide receiver Randy Moss wasn't catching touchdown passes, they taunted him. They came roaring out of the locker room to shred one of the league's best defenses on scoring drives to start the game and the second half.

Domenik Hixon, making his debut as a kick returner, took a kickoff 74 yards for a touchdown.

In the final minutes, the Giants (10-6), refusing to roll over, drove to a touchdown that was meaningless because the game was all but decided, and meaningful because it gave them momentum as they headed to Tampa Bay to play the Buccaneers in an NFC wild-card game.

The Patriots, who had downplayed the historical significance of the game all week, hugged each other from the field to the visitors locker room. They gave out game balls like M&M's, including one to owner Robert Kraft.

They are the first team to finish a regular season unbeaten since the 1972 Miami Dolphins finished 14-0. The Dolphins won

three postseason games, including the Super Bowl, to complete their season 17-0.

Of course, the Patriots know they must win a title — their fourth in seven years — for this to have lasting meaning.

"That was some way to finish the season," coach Bill Belichick said. "It's a great feeling. Now's the time to take a day or two, I think, and appreciate what this team has done. But at the same time, we have to look forward again. We're going to take a little bit of time to enjoy this one and feel good about what we accomplished. But pretty soon we need to turn a page and move on."

For a while, it appeared all those Giants fans who had sold their tickets to the deep-pocketed New Englanders had lured them into an ambush. But in the end, the Patriots took control in the fourth quarter, rallied from a 12-point deficit and added this victory to the list of other near-misses — against the Colts, Eagles and Ravens.

With nothing at stake for them — their wild-card game against the Buccaneers already set — the Giants shoved their shoulders against the doors of history and

LEFT: Giants wide receiver Domenik Hixon returns a first-half kickoff for a touchdown.
Photo by Chris Faytok

ABOVE: Giants fan Chris Craft, from Yonkers, NY, with Big Blue Road Crew, serves up some tasty hamburgers to football fans before the Giants game against the New England Patriots at Giants Stadium. *Photo by Saed Hindash*

RIGHT: Giants head coach Tom Coughlin roams the sidelines during the first half. *Photo by Chris Faytok*

held for as long as they could.

The Patriots didn't take the lead for good until early in the fourth quarter, when Moss, after dropping a possible touchdown heave on the previous play, caught one on a do-over. With a 2-point conversion tacked on, the history-making 65-yarder from Brady gave the Super Bowl favorites a 31-28 lead with 11:06 left.

The touchdown pass, the second scoring hookup of the game for the pair, gave single-season records to Brady for touchdown passes (50) and touchdown receptions for Moss (23). In the victory, the Patriots also set a record for most points in a season.

When the Patriots intercepted Manning with 9:53 remaining and turned that into a touchdown run by Laurence Maroney for a 10-point lead, the Giants still didn't pull their starters. And Manning drove them to a touchdown on a 3-yard pass to Plaxico Burress with 1:04 left in the game. An onside kick failed.

"I told the team there were no negatives from this, only positives," coach Tom Coughlin said. "We had everything to gain and nothing to lose."

And, injuries aside, they probably gained a lot. Coughlin, who could have benched his best players rather than risk them to injury and bruised egos, instead played them. And the gamble was rewarded when Manning played one of his best games of

OPPOSITE: Plaxico Burress makes a catch on the Giants first drive. *Photo by Andrew Mills*

LEFT: Kevin Boss catches a touchdown pass late in the first half. *Photo by Andrew Mills*

RIGHT: Brandon Jacobs is brought down by Richard Seymour of the Patriots. *Photo by Saed Hindash*

OPPOSITE: With the capacity crowd on its feet, Eli Manning scrambles for yardage near the end zone. *Photo by Andrew Mills*

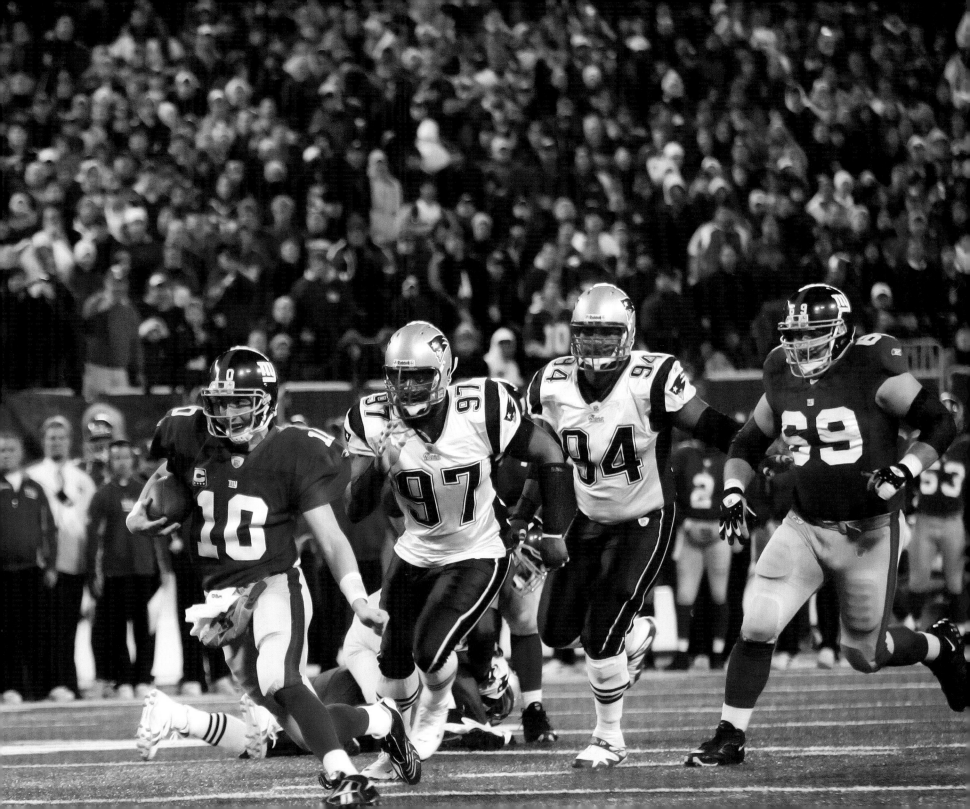

the season against the toughest defense he has faced.

"The final outcome was not the most important thing for us," Manning said. "We wanted to come out and execute our game plan, make some plays, and we did that. We've struggled lately, but we ran the ball and spread it around in the passing game. We haven't done that in a while."

The Giants, after stunning the world — come on, admit it, you were stunned — by taking a 21-16 halftime lead, padded it to 28-16 with a 60-yard drive on their first possession of the second half. Manning capped the drive with a 19-yard touch-down pass, on a rollout, to Plaxico Burress in the right corner of the end zone.

The Patriots, playing for those tell-my-grandkids memories, scored on a 6-yard run by Maroney, who slipped through the arms of cornerback Aaron Ross with four minutes left in the third quarter to cut the deficit to 28-23. Moss's long touchdown and conversion gave the Pats a 31-28 lead.

Coughlin, facing a 10-point deficit after a valiant effort, could have pulled his start-ers, but he left them in. On third down, Manning found Burress, who in his post-game praised his teammates ("We didn't back down"), ripped the referees enough to warrant a fine ("Some of the worst of-ficiating I've seen in my eight years," he said), and took a shot at the Patriots ("They cheap-shot you and try to draw you into penalties").

LEFT: Domenik Hixon returns a kickoff for a touchdown during the second half. *Photo by Chris Faytok*

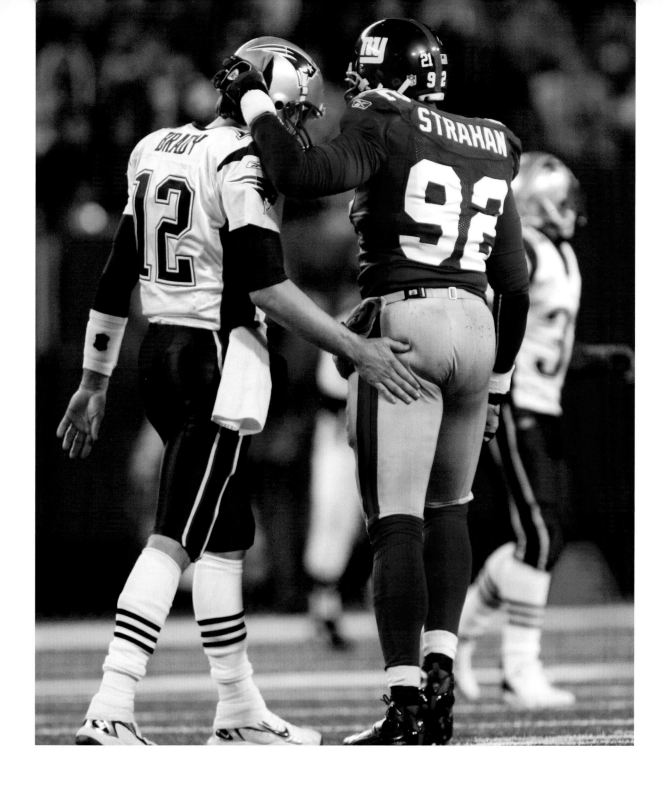

So much for his reverence toward history.

As the Patriots celebrated and sighed, the Giants were patting themselves on the back for hanging tough. Losing wasn't the end of the world.

"We took our best shot at the best team in the league," linebacker Antonio Pierce said. "Everyone argued about what we should do. We did what we said we would: We played hard and gave them everything we had."

All of which led Manning to conclude: "We're ready for Tampa." ■

PREVIOUS LEFT: Giants wide receiver Steve Smith tries to get past Patriots safety Rodney Harrison after a reception during the second half. *Photo by Chris Faytok*

PREVIOUS RIGHT: Giants linebacker Reggie Torbor sacks Patriots quarterback Tom Brady *Photo by Chris Faytok*

OPPOSITE: Michael Strahan slaps the top of Tom Brady's helmet as the Giants put pressure on him in the third quarter. *Photo by Saed Hindash*

LEFT: Tom Brady and Michael Strahan exchange pats during the second half. *Photo by Andrew Mills*

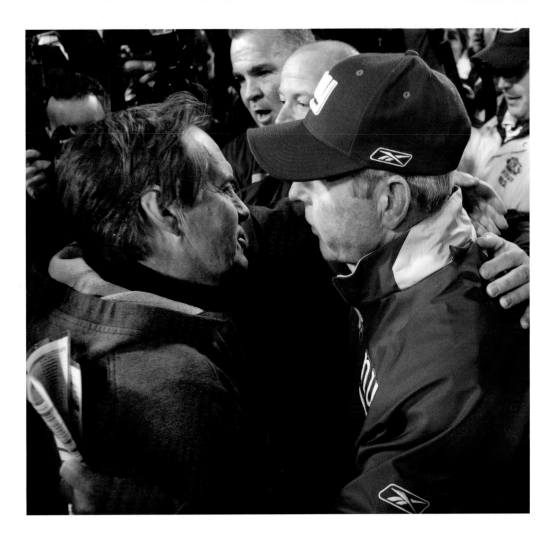

ABOVE: Patriots coach Bill Belichick, left, and Giants coach Tom Coughlin hug after the game. The Patriots won 38-35, finishing the regular season with a record of 16-0. *Photo by Scott Lituchy*

LEFT: Patriots quarterback Tom Brady looks to shake hands with Giants quarterback Eli Manning after the final regular season game.
Photo by Chris Faytok

BUCING THE TREND
NFC WILDCARD: GIANTS 24, BUCS 14

By Mike Garafolo

Amani Toomer looked around Raymond James Stadium at the pirate ship, the palm trees and the red and pewter seats. It all reminded him that this is where the Giants' four-game playoff losing streak began when they were blown out by the Ravens in Super Bowl XXXV.

After a 24-14 wildcard victory against the Buccaneers, the streak is over. Tom Coughlin has his first postseason win as the Giants coach. Eli Manning has his first as an NFL quarterback. And the team is headed to the second weekend of the playoffs — they will be on the road against the Dallas Cowboys — after losing in the first round the past two years.

"Our organization lost something the last time we were here (in the playoffs)," Toomer said while dressing in the same slanted-roofed locker room that housed a

LEFT: The Giants' Brandon Jacobs scores a touchdown in the second quarter.
Photo by Tim Farrell

disappointed bunch of Giants seven years ago. "Hopefully, today, we got a little bit of it back."

One thing they're absolutely getting back is their coach. It might never be known what another first-round exit would have meant for Coughlin's job security, but taking this team farther than last year is confirmation progress has been made.

It was done the way many expected it couldn't: Without retired running back Tiki Barber, whose only appearance on the field came more than an hour after the game, when he chased his sons A.J. and Chason all over the field.

Without Barber, a Pro Bowl running back but a dividing force in the locker room, Coughlin has moved his team forward.

"It's all about our team. It's not anything about me," he said. "It's about our players, and our players played well. I just think there was a real solid feeling that everyone was going to make a great effort, nobody wanted to let the other guy down."

Or their coach.

"It was a team win," said right guard

Chris Snee, Coughlin's son-in-law. "But, hey, if it gets everyone off his back, I'm happy for him."

Manning also silenced a few detractors — including Bucs cornerback and Tiki's brother Ronde Barber, who said the fourth-year quarterback "can be had." Against the NFL's No. 1 pass defense this season, Manning pump-faked, scrambled and ad-libbed his way to 20 completions in 27 attempts for 185 yards, two touchdowns and, most importantly, no interceptions.

All of which led Toomer to yell, "He could be had, though," while running past Manning on his way to the winning locker room.

"We've been in the playoffs the last three seasons, and I haven't played particularly well in the two games before," Manning said. "To come in here and play well, give our team a chance to win the game and make some big plays, that was quite a situation to be in."

The defense kept them in that situation despite allowing yet another early touchdown. Coordinator Steve Spagnuolo made adjustments once again and the best pass

ABOVE: Eli Manning speaks with offensive coordinator Kevin Gilbride in the second half. *Photo by Andrew Mills*

LEFT: R.W. McQuarters dances for fans during pregame warmups. *Photo by Andrew Mills*

ABOVE: Giants quarterback Eli Manning and his teammates emerge from the tunnel to begin the first half.

Photo by Andrew Mills

LEFT: A lone Giants fan in a sea of Bucs fans celebrates
a Giants' touchdown in the fourth quarter.

Photo by Tim Farrell

rush in the league was all over Bucs quarterback Jeff Garcia (23-for-39 for 207 yards, one touchdown and two interceptions), who had beaten the Giants twice before in the playoffs. The front four might have only sacked Garcia once, but they pressured and hit him more than a dozen times.

Still, the real key to the defensive performance was the secondary, which was without injured starting cornerback Sam Madison. In his place, third-year corner Corey Webster played perhaps the best game of his career. He recovered a fumble on the opening kickoff of the second half to set up a field goal that made it 17-7, then had an interception in the end zone on a pass intended for Joey Galloway on the next drive.

"I think they played better as a secondary than maybe what we gave them credit for," Garcia said.

The Bucs' defense certainly gave the Giants' running game credit, stacking as many as eight defenders near the line. That was an effective strategy until rookie running back Ahmad Bradshaw slashed his way to 38 yards on seven carries during a 92-yard drive that began in the third quarter and ended almost seven minutes into the fourth quarter, when Manning pumped toward tight end Kevin Boss and hit Toomer (seven catches, 74 yards) for a

LEFT: Eli Manning directs traffic.
Photo by Tim Farrell

OPPOSITE: Amani Toomer takes a knee in the end zone after his touchdown catch.
Photo by Andrew Mills

PREVIOUS LEFT: Giants wide receiver Plaxico Burress eyes the Bucs' Ronde Barber as he runs with the ball after a catch in the fourth quarter. *Photo by Andrew Mills*

PREVIOUS RIGHT: Ahmad Bradshaw gestures to the crowd during a timeout in the fourth quarter. *Photo by Tim Farrell*

ABOVE: A Giants fan gives it to the Bucs fans after the Giants scored a touchdown in the fourth quarter. *Photo by Tim Farrell*

RIGHT: Ahmad Bradshaw drives for extra yards despite getting his helmet knocked off. *Photo by Tim Farrell*

OPPOSITE: Burress gets physical with Barber. *Photo by Andrew Mills*

ABOVE: A Giants fan shows her support in the second half. *Photo by Andrew Mills*

RIGHT: Giants running back Brandon Jacobs screams "Thank You" to fans as he leaves the field with his arms raised after the Giants defeated the Buccaneers. *Photo by Andrew Mills*

4-yard touchdown.

Wide receiver Plaxico Burress celebrated the score by tugging an imaginary truck horn while facing fans behind the end zone.

"That's the 'Big Rig.' The running game," Burress said. "No stopping it."

The Giants now believe there's no stopping them. They're over that first-round hump; the pressure is off their coach and quarterback ... for now. They're playing well in all phases of the game on their way to Texas for their third meeting of the season with the Cowboys.

And seven years after losing their playoff winning ways in this building, they've finally gotten them back.

"Everybody said it's been since (2001), and that seemed like yesterday," 15-year defensive end Michael Strahan said. "And then, I realized it's 2008." ■

PREVIOUS LEFT: R.W. McQuarters makes an interception in the fourth quarter, just getting his feet in bounds.
Photo by Tim Farrell

PREVIOUS RIGHT: Eli Manning completes a pass to tight end Kevin Boss in the fourth quarter.
Photo by Andrew Mills

LEFT: Giants offensive guard Chris Snee raises his arms as the final seconds of the game tick off.
Photo by Tim Farrell

TEXAS ROUNDUP
NFC PLAYOFF: GIANTS 21, COWBOYS 17

By Mike Garafolo

Tom Coughlin wrapped up his press conference, turned away from the microphone and took one step toward the edge of the podium, where he was met by Amani Toomer.

What ensued was a scene that, three years ago, was perhaps the most improbable, unthinkable thing that could ever happen.

Toomer hugged his coach.

And not a one-armed, "Hey, congratulations," kind of hug. A back-slapping, swaying, bear hug of an embrace. The kind

of hug, with Toomer still in all of his pads, that looked like it hurt Coughlin.

Chances are, he didn't feel a thing.

Not after his group of All-Joes beat the All-Pros in a game that defied history and logic. The Giants, with their relentless pass rush, strolled into Texas Stadium and beat the Cowboys, 21-17. It was the first time since the NFL went to a 12-team playoff format in 1990 that the NFC's No. 1 seed lost in the divisional round. It was also only the seventh time in 18 chances since the 1970 AFL-NFL merger that a team won a playoff game against an opponent it lost to twice during the regular season.

And so, the Giants will be headed to Green Bay to face the Packers in the NFC Championship Game. And they'll be hugging their coach the whole way there.

"A couple years ago it would have been hard for me to imagine that," said Toomer, who sparked the victory with a 52-yard

touchdown catch in the first quarter on which he broke two tackles, then added a touchdown to tie the game late in the second quarter. "Not to say anything too wrong, it's just the way it was.

"But right now the way he is ... he's going to do anything he can to help this team, anything he feels that's right to win."

Now, he has the results to justify the methods. A year after nearly losing his job, Coughlin can pretty much name his price.

But that was last week's story line after the win over the Buccaneers. This week's centers around a team that could actually — gasp! — make the Super Bowl.

One mention of playing in that game yesterday caused middle linebacker Antonio Pierce to get a little choked up during his postgame press conference, while Cowboys wide receiver Terrell Owens cried a different kind of tears down the hall.

Pierce later admitted his eyes started to

LEFT: Cowboys running back Marion Barber is gang tackled by Giants (left to right) Gibril Wilson, James Butler, Antonio Pierce and R.W. McQuarters in the first half. *Photo by Andrew Mills*

FOLLOWING LEFT: Giants fans take photos as the team warms up before the game. *Photo by Chris Faytok*

FOLLOWING RIGHT: Eli Manning talks with head coach Tom Coughlin before the game. *Photo by Chris Faytok*

get watery as soon as tenth-year veteran cornerback R.W. McQuarters intercepted Tony Romo's fourth-down pass to Terry Glenn in the end zone with nine seconds left in the game.

"I didn't ever want to cry (over) football before," said Pierce, who began his career as an undrafted free agent with the Redskins in 2001. "But that's the best moment I've ever had in football."

It was also Eli Manning's. On a day big brother Peyton and the Colts had already lost, the younger Manning played another solid game at the stadium in which he suffered a shoulder injury on opening night. Yesterday he completed 12 of his 18 passes for 163 yards and two touchdowns, never losing his rhythm despite standing on the sideline and watching the Cowboys put together drives of 20 and 14 plays, which ate up a combined 18 minutes, 35 seconds

LEFT: Giants quarterback Eli Manning hangs in the pocket despite pressure during the first half.
Photo by Chris Faytok

OPPOSITE: Giants running back Ahmad Bradshaw eludes a tackle in the second half.
Photo by Chris Faytok

of game clock.

The 20-play drive, on which the Cowboys converted six third downs, ended with a 1-yard touchdown run by Marion Barber that gave Dallas a 14-7 lead with 1:07 left in the first half. Manning responded by completing four of his seven passes on the next drive, which he capped with a 4-yard touchdown throw to Toomer over the middle.

"They had all the momentum. They had a long drive, the defense was gassed," Manning said. "To get a touchdown there, to tie it up before halftime, that was a big momentum-builder for our team."

As was a stop on third-and-12 on the first drive of the second half. With Owens streaking across the middle of the field, Romo threw high and over his head, forcing Dallas to settle for a field goal and a

OPPOSITE: Giants cornerback Aaron Ross tackles Cowboys wide receiver Patrick Crayton for a loss during the first half. *Photo by Chris Faytok*

LEFT: Giants linebacker Kawika Mitchell stands up Dallas running back Marion Barber in the first half. *Photo by Andrew Mills*

ABOVE: Giants cornerback R.W. McQuarters on the sidelines in the first half. *Photo by Chris Faytok*

RIGHT: Giants linebacker Antonio Pierce (58) pounces on Cowboys quarterback Tony Romo along with fellow linebacker Kawika Mitchell in the first half. *Photo by Andrew Mills*

OPPOSITE: Giants wide receiver Amani Toomer scores the team's first touchdown. *Photo by Chris Faytok*

three-point lead. At that point, the Giants defense knew it had Romo rattled and had started to wear Barber down. The next drive was a three-and-out for the Cowboys.

McQuarters then returned a punt 25 yards to the Dallas 37. Manning hit Toomer on a hook to the left side, found Steve Smith on the right side and, on third-and-6, connected with the rookie receiver again on a key 11-yard hook. Two plays later, Brandon Jacobs scored the game-winning touchdown and celebrated by firing the football into the play clock behind the end zone.

It was a sign of disrespect toward the only stadium in which they had lost a road game this season.

"We had a big sign posted: 'Warriors 9-1 coming in here,'" Coughlin said of the

OPPOSITE: Giants wide receiver Steve Smith goes up to haul in a key 21-yard reception late in the second quarter. *Photo by Andrew Mills*

LEFT: Giants wide receiver Amani Toomer dives into the end zone for the game-tying touchdown late in the second quarter. *Photo by Andrew Mills*

ABOVE: Giants fan and NJ native Joe Ruback reacts to the Giants' touchdown in the second half. *Photo by Andrew Mills*

LEFT: Linebacker Kawika Mitchell (55) and Fred Robbins (98) swarm Cowboys quarterback Tony Romo for a sack in the second half.

Photo by Chris Faytok

team's record away from home. "And we were able to win on the road again."

How about 10-1? Maybe. After losing here in Week 1, they lost to Green Bay at home seven days later. This time, they're headed to Wisconsin — while Romo is free to go back to Mexico for a couple of months if he'd like.

As Texas native Willie Nelson once sang — in a tune reprised yesterday by Giants assistant video director Carmen Pizzano as he walked through the locker room — the Giants are headed "on the road again."

Perhaps it's the "road" to the Super Bowl. ∎

OPPOSITE: Giants defensive end Osi Umenyiora pressures Tony Romo. *Photo by Chris Faytok*

LEFT: Quarterback Eli Manning celebrates a touchdown run by Brandon Jacobs during the second half.
Photo by Chris Faytok

THIS SPREAD: Giants corner Corey Webster breaks up a long pass intended for the Cowboys'
Terrell Owens in the fourth quarter. *Photo by Andrew Mills*

ABOVE: Giants wide receiver Amani Toomer talks with TV reporters after giving his gloves to servicemen in the front row following the game. *Photo by Chris Faytok*

LEFT: Giants defensive end Michael Strahan (92) celebrates with R.W. McQuarters (25), who picked off the last pass of the game. *Photo by Chris Faytok*

THIRD TYNES A CHARM
NFC CHAMPIONSHIP: GIANTS 23, PACKERS 20

By Mike Garafolo

Once the ball cleared the uprights, Lawrence Tynes turned and sprinted between the hash marks to the far end zone and the tunnel that led to a warm locker room. Within minutes, his teammates would follow.

There, the Giants hugged one another, red-faced and practically frost-bitten after their thrilling 23-20 overtime victory against the Packers in the NFC Championship Game at Lambeau Field.

While Michael Strahan cradled the George Halas Trophy and spoke of the benefits of skipping training camp, Osi Umenyiora jumped up and down with his hands on Justin Tuck's shoulders and yelled, "Super Bowl! Super Bowl!"

Owners John Mara and Steve and Jon Tisch, who gave Tom Coughlin a vote of confidence and a contract extension a year ago, spoke lovingly of their late fathers. And almost every player stopped to lean over and hug Lt. Col. Greg Gadson, a

double amputee whose survival story was a source of inspiration.

This group of underdogs — with Mara and the rest of the Giants brain trust were mauling each other in a celebratory hug few could have even fathomed when that call was placed on a hot summer day.

The Giants — a team with a seemingly lame-duck coach, a quarterback with no guts, a retired running back bashing them from the studio booth and a defense that couldn't stop anybody (including the Packers) through the first two weeks of the season — are going to the Super Bowl. There, they'll get their second chance to derail the Patriots' perfect season.

"I'm happy for so many other people that it hasn't struck me yet, really," said coach Tom Coughlin, who is in the middle of one of the greatest single-season turn-arounds for any coach in NFL history. And after getting a vote of confidence from John Mara and Steve and Jon Tisch when things were at their lowest last year at this time, Coughlin took time to remember their late fathers, "I was asked the other day if ever I think of Mr. Mara and Mr. Tisch. Yeah, we do. I'm happy for them as well."

The Giants are happy to have their coach. And to have another shot at New England.

Just like Tynes and cornerback Corey Webster, who set up the game-winning kick with an interception one week after dropping an easy one against the Cowboys, the Giants will get an opportunity for another make-good moment.

"The road of redemption, that's for sure," center Shaun O'Hara said of the wins over Dallas and Green Bay, who combined to beat the Giants three times in the regular season. "Hopefully, we can continue that."

They almost got run off the road yesterday on three occasions.

With 6:53 remaining in the fourth quarter and the score tied at 20, Tynes lined up for a 43-yard field goal. He missed it wide left.

The Packers then had a pair of three-and-outs. But veteran Giants cornerback R.W. McQuarters, who had sealed last week's win over Dallas with an interception, fumbled on a punt return. Luckily for McQuarters — who lost a fumble on an interception return earlier — and the Giants, the frozen ball skidded past Packers

---

LEFT: Shaun O'Hara (left) embraces Michael Strahan and says, 'Thank you for not retiring!' as they embrace after the NFC Championship. *Photo by Andrew Mills*

Jarrett Bush and Brady Poppinga and into the grasp of Domenik Hixon.

The Giants drove to the Packers' 18-yard line for what should have been an easy 36-yarder for Tynes to win it with four seconds left. But again, he pulled it wide left.

"We had a little bit of a high snap," holder Jeff Feagles said. "The conditions were very difficult today. The balls were very, very hard."

The ball — and the Giants defense — seemed to give Favre trouble late in the game. He completed only two of his last seven passes for 12 yards.

And in overtime, he tried to force a pass to wide receiver Donald Driver, who had a 90-yard touchdown in the second quarter.

Webster jammed Driver at the line and picked off the pass for his second interception of the postseason.

"We kind of figured that's who he was going to go to in a crucial time of the game," Webster said.

With the ball at the Packers' 34-yard line, the Giants knew they weren't close enough. Not after Tynes' first two kicks,

---

OPPOSITE: Pre-game flag ceremony at the NFC Championship Game. *Photo by Chris Faytok*

TOP: Bikini-clad Packers fans brave the minus-4 degree weather. *Photo by Andrew Mills*

BOTTOM: Red-faced Tom Coughlin in the first half. *Photo by Andrew Mills*

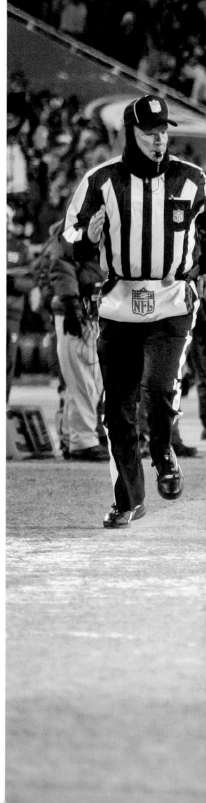

ABOVE: Giants quarterback Eli Manning tries to keep warm on the sidelines during the second half. *Photo by Chris Faytok*

RIGHT: The Packers' Koren Robinson and Tramon Williams recover a fumble in front of Chase Blackburn on a Giants kickoff in the second quarter. *Photo by Tim Farrell*

OPPOSITE: The Packers' Donald Driver high-steps past a diving Corey Webster on the way to a 90-yard touchdown to put the Packers up 7-6. *Photo by Andrew Mills*

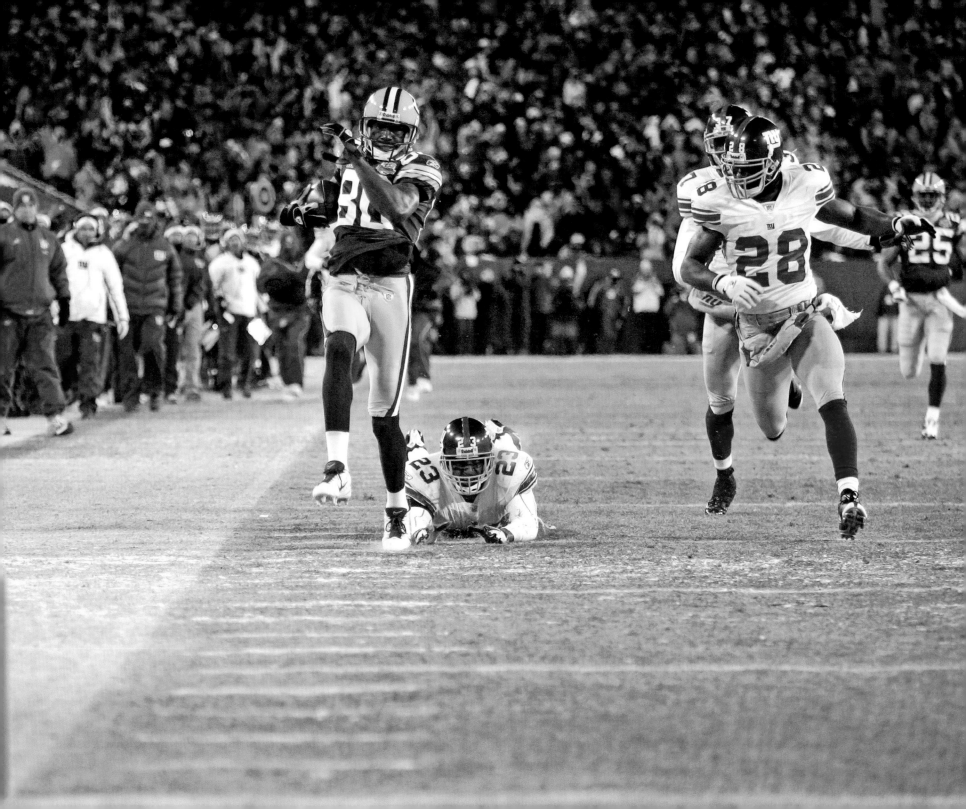

ABOVE: Giants defensive end Justin Tuck helps up Packers quarterback Brett Favre during the first half. *Photo by Chris Faytok*

RIGHT: Plaxico Burress makes a leaping catch in front of a big cushion from Packers cornerback Al Harris. *Photo by Chris Faytok*

OPPOSITE: Line of scrimmage in the first half of the NFC Championship Game between the Giants and the Packers at Lambeau Field. *Photo by Chris Faytok*

FOLLOWING LEFT: The Giants' Aaron Ross upends the Packers' James Jones to break up a pass in the first quarter. *Photo by Tim Farrell*

FOLLOWING RIGHT: Packers quarterback Brett Favre takes the snap in the first half. *Photo by Chris Faytok/The Star-Ledger*

ABOVE: Giants head coach Tom Coughlin cheers for his team after a third-quarter touchdown. *Photo by Tim Farrell*

LEFT Giants defensive tackle Jay Alford tries to get past Packers offensive tackle Mark Tauscher as Brett Favre looks to throw. *Photo by Chris Faytok*

FOLLOWING LEFT: Ahmad Bradshaw carries the ball in the second half. *Photo by Andrew Mills*

FOLLOWING RIGHT: Amani Toomer gets both feet in as he catches a long pass in the second half to set up the Giants' second touchdown. *Photo by Andrew Mills*

which brought to mind Jay Feely's three missed field goals in Seattle in 2005. And after a shaky start to the season in which he missed two extra points, Tynes had yet to be tested since being acquired in a trade from the Chiefs last May.

The Giants moved the ball only 5 yards and Coughlin, who was jumping up and down like an excited child after Webster's interception, thought about punting or going for it on fourth down. But he saw an eager field-goal group and gave Tynes one more chance.

After the game, he would joke with Tynes, "We just needed to move the ball back for you. We were too close before."

At the time, though, Coughlin was extremely nervous. It wasn't until the ball sailed through the uprights that Coughlin, who was finally headed to the Super Bowl after two losses in the AFC Championship Game with the Jaguars, could throw his hands up in victory.

As for Tynes, he sprinted right between the hash marks to the far end zone and into the tunnel. He would do his celebrating in the locker room.

"I spent enough time in that damn cold," Tynes said.

So did the rest of the Giants, who were red-faced and exhausted in the locker room. Only the thought of heading to Arizona in a week could keep them warm.

"I'll play in negative-50 to play in 70," said Giants running back Brandon Jacobs, exaggerating a bit for effect. "And that's what we did." ∎

PREVIOUS LEFT: Giants running back Ahmad Bradshaw is about to fire the football against the end zone wall after running the ball into the end zone, but the play would be called back for holding. *Photo by Chris Faytok*

PREVIOUS RIGHT: Giants corner R.W. McQuarters fumbles an interception back to the Packers in the fourth quarter.
Photo by Andrew Mills

RIGHT: Fans are bundled up for the cold. *Photo by Tim Farrell*

BELOW: Giants fans celebrate during the second half. *Photo by Chris Faytok*

OPPOSITE: Corey Webster makes a key interception in overtime that leads to the Giants' game-winning field goal to win the NFC Championship.
Photo by Andrew Mills

RIGHT: Giants place kicker Lawrence Tynes celebrates his game-winning field goal in overtime. *Photo by Tim Farrell*

OPPOSITE: Eli Manning celebrates with fans after the game. *Photo by Chris Faytok*

NOW THAT'S PERFECT

HISTORIC FINAL DRIVE LEADS GIANTS TO SUPER BOWL XLII VICTORY

By Mike Garafolo

GLENDALE, Ariz. – There was confetti stuck to their sweaty heads, blood on their tight-fitting undershirts and tears in their eyes. The dream season, which often resembled a nightmare, had ended in the most unlikely fashion — a 17-14 victory over the New England Patriots in Super Bowl XLII.

Eli Manning received a hug and an "I love you" from his brother Peyton. His father Archie told him the team "is going to have a great party," while his mother Olivia, knowing her son's penchant for a little karaoke, asked him if he knew how to sing "New York, New York."

Inside the locker room, Antonio Pierce sought out all of the doubters in the media one by one, asking them how it felt to be wrong.

Osi Umenyiora grabbed wide receivers coach Mike Sullivan, who must have taught David Tyree how to catch a ball on the side of his head, and playfully asked, "David Tyree? Geez."

Michael Strahan hugged anybody and everybody he could find.

Tom Coughlin did one interview. Then two, three and even four.

Wide receiver Plaxico Burress, he of the ankle and knee injuries, came out of the training room with his left shoulder wrapped.

And Manning — the MVP of the game — received a huge ovation from his teammates, coaches and family members of all those involved with the team.

Go figure.

Actually, there is no figuring what happened here at University of Phoenix Stadium. For those inside that locker room who never doubted, the sight of Burress catching the 13-yard, game-winning touchdown with 35 seconds remaining to beat the previously perfect Patriots was something even they couldn't comprehend.

"To come and play a team that's 18-0 and beat them," president and COO John Mara said, "I haven't accepted the fact that it's real yet. Maybe I will tomorrow."

Added executive vice president and chairman Steve Tisch: "The Cowboys might be America's Team, but the Giants are America's Dream."

The dream could have ended at any moment, most notably when Manning was in

---

LEFT: Eli Manning hoists the Vince Lombardi Trophy with head coach Tom Coughlin by his side. *Photo by Andrew Mills*

139

OPPOSITE: Eli Manning is surrounded by the media at the University of Phoenix Stadium. *Photo by Chris Faytok*

LEFT: Michael Strahan crashes a TV appearance by fellow defensive end Osi Umenyiora during media day festivities. *Photo by Andrew Mills*

BELOW: Safety Michael Johnson is asked whether he thinks Eli Manning would marry the TV Azteca reporter. *Photo by Chris Faytok*

the grasp of two defenders — seemingly a second away from falling face-down into the grass — on third-and-five on the fateful final drive.

"Nobody brought me down," said Manning, who completed 19 of 34 passes for 255 yards, two touchdowns and one interception. "I just tried to stay small."

He did — and Manning made a big play when he somehow wriggled free and tossed the ball downfield toward Tyree, of all people. The Montclair native, who had four catches in the regular season, was about to make the biggest of his career — a 32-yard completion that he pressed against the side of his helmet with 59 seconds left.

Four plays later, Burress made a double move on Patriots cornerback Ellis Hobbs, trotted to the left side of the end zone and made an easy catch a few minutes after Manning had overthrown him on a similarly easy play.

LEFT: The scene outside at University of Phoenix Stadium on the eve of Super Bowl XLII. *Photo by Andrew Mills*

BELOW: R.W. McQuarters, left, and Corey Webster get the crowd fired up. *Photo by Chris Faytok*

Burress, who didn't practice all week, said the Giants had noticed on film Hobbs "stopped his feet" when in coverage at the goal line.

"I gave him a slant move," Burress said, "and he stopped his feet."

Fitting, because the Patriots' quest for perfection was stopped.

Forever, they will be known as the 18-1 team that couldn't close the deal while the Giants (14-6) will go down in history as the team that, well, saved history and preserved the 1972 Miami Dolphins' claim to being the only undefeated Super Bowl champion.

The Giants will be known as the team that refused to quit — from the moment they were 0-2 all the way until Randy Moss' touchdown with 2:42 remaining and the extra point gave the Patriots a three-point lead.

The dream appeared to be over. Until the Giants hit the snooze button and Manning led them to victory with five completions for 77 yards on the game-winning drive, which went 12 plays and 83 yards.

"You say he became a man. I don't know if he did that on that drive," said defensive end Justin Tuck, who had two sacks and a forced fumble. "He became an elder statesman."

Said Burress: "Nobody gave us a shot. Can somebody give our defense some credit?"

Uh, they have been. And after Steve Spagnuolo's unit held the Patriots' offense to a season-low in points, they deserve all the credit they can get over the next few days, weeks and months.

The Giants were all over Tom Brady (29-for-48 for 266 yards and one touchdown) with their relentless pass rush — they sacked Brady five times — and their

---

RIGHT: Fans in the upper deck are dwarfed by a Giants poster.
Photo by Chris Faytok

BELOW: Michael Strahan gets the team pumped. *Photo by William Perlman*

secondary did a terrific job limiting the Patriots' attempts down the field. Add to that, the Pats gained just 45 yards on the ground.

So New England settled for a short-passing game that set the kind of tempo the Giants wanted. After all, they had lost a 38-35 track meet against the Patriots on Dec. 29 at Giants Stadium. This game allowed the Giants to hang in there, keep pressuring Brady and trade punts long enough to make a big play to break it open.

That play was a 45-yard catch-and-run by rookie

tight end Kevin Boss early in the fourth quarter. It was called "137 comeback," but offensive coordinator Kevin Gilbride added a "Y seam" for Boss because he noticed Patriots safety Rodney Harrison was cheating toward

---

BELOW: Osi Umenyiora and Michael Strahan wait to come out of the tunnel before the game. *Photo by Andrew Mills*

RIGHT: Brandon Jacobs drives through the line during the first half. *Photo by Andrew Mills*

the line of scrimmage.

"We didn't practice that all week," Boss said.

A few plays later, Tyree etched his name into Super Bowl history with a 5-yard touchdown in front of cornerback Asante Samuel that made it 10-7 Giants. It was Tyree's first touchdown since Dec. 10, 2006, against the Carolina Panthers.

But it was nothing like his reception later in the fourth quarter.

"That might be the greatest catch in Super Bowl history," Coughlin said.

And the dream? Well, it's the greatest they've ever dreamt.

"To have guys that have played in this league for so long and have been great pros, to have them have the opportunity to wear that ring," said Coughlin, the 61-year-old, 12-year veteran coach, "that's the best feeling of all." ∎

ABOVE: James Butler tackles Laurence Maroney. *Photo by John Munson*

RIGHT: Steve Smith makes a leaping catch in front of cornerback Randall Gay. *Photo by Chris Faytok*

FOLLOWING LEFT: Michael Strahan gets to the ball as he deflects the pass by Tom Brady. *Photo by Tim Farrell*

FOLLOWING RIGHT: Tom Brady watches as the Osi Umenyiora recovers his fumble after the Pats' quarterback was sacked late in the first half. *Photo by Andrew Mills*

ABOVE: Steve Smith watches as the ball bounces off his hands to the Ellis Hobbs. *Photo by Tim Farrell*

LEFT: Eli Manning passes the ball as Steve Smith looks for the reception during the first half. *Photo by Chris Faytok*

FOLLOWING LEFT: Eli Manning looks on as Rodney Harrison celebrates. *Photo by Chris Faytok*

FOLLOWING RIGHT: Giants fans send a message to Patriots' head coach Bill Belichick. *Photo by Andrew Mills*

ABOVE: Ahmad Bradshaw would be called for an illegal batting of the ball on this play as linebacker Mike Vrabel pursues in the first half. *Photo by Chris Faytok*

LEFT: Brady is hit by Barry Cofield and Osi Umenyiora in the first half. *Photo by Tim Farrell*

FOLLOWING LEFT: Giants fans show their support during the first quarter. *Photo by Chris Faytok*

FOLLOWING RIGHT: Ahmad Bradshaw runs with the ball during the first quarter. *Photo by Chris Faytok*

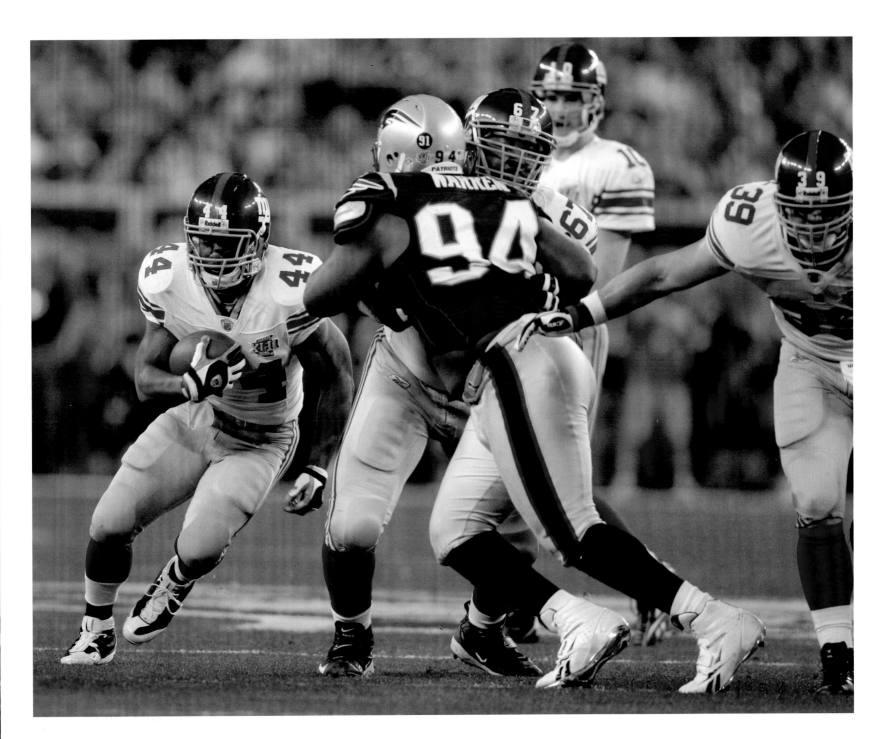

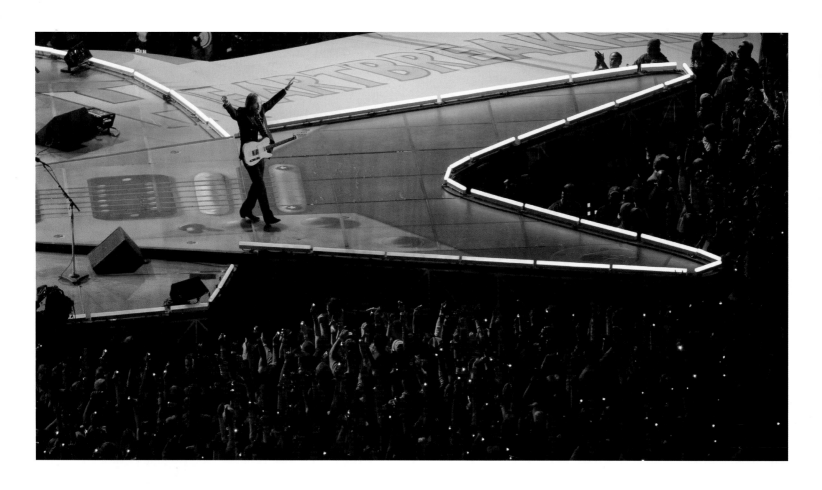

ABOVE: Tom Petty performs at halftime. *Photo by John Munson*

RIGHT: Petty performed some of his classics for the millions of people that watched the game. *Photo by John Munson*

FOLLOWING LEFT: Tom Coughlin barks from the sidelines during the second half. *Photo by Chris Faytok*

FOLLOWING RIGHT: Tom Brady is sacked by Michael Strahan during the third quarter. *Photo by Chris Faytok*

167

PREVIOUS LEFT: Steve Smith makes a catch as he's upended by Brandon Meriweather. *Photo by Chris Faytok*

PREVIOUS RIGHT: Kevin Boss makes a big reception in the fourth quarter as he is pursued by Adalius Thomas and Rodney Harrison. *Photo by Chris Faytok*

OPPOSITE: David Tyree is mobbed by teammates after his fourth-quarter touchdown. *Photo by John Munson*

LEFT: Wes Welker runs after a catch as the Giants' defense, including free safety James Butler and cornerback Aaron Ross close in during the third quarter. *Photo by Chris Faytok*

FOLLOWING LEFT: Osi Umenyiora looks for some help from Justin Tuck as Tom Brady is on his knees in the second half.
Photo by Chris Faytok

FOLLOWING RIGHT: Giants fans in the front row look on as a wide open Randy Moss beats cornerback Corey Webster for a fourth-quarter touchdown catch. *Photo by Chris Faytok*

THE CATCH

Tyree's big fourth-quarter grab could be best ever in Super Bowl history

By Brad Parks

GLENDALE, Ariz. – There are some things you can't explain. This is how David Tyree began talking about the catch of his life.

He was sitting on interview podium No. 3 at this point — even he admitted he was probably the least likely guy to get a postgame Super Bowl interview slot — and his uniform was still plastered to his body with sweat, still smelling of grass.

Super Bowl XLII, which the Giants had taken from the Patriots, 17-14, was over by about a half hour at this point, and Tyree was still shaking his head.

"Some things just don't make sense," Tyree said. "And that catch was one of them."

To set the scene: It was third down and five, 75 seconds left in the game, with the Giants four points down, 56 yards away from the end zone,

and two plays away from being footnotes to the Patriots' perfect season.

Giants quarterback Eli Manning dropped back and was immediately swarmed by the Patriots' pass rush.

"I felt some hands on me," Manning said later. By "some," of course, he meant about 11.

But somehow, Manning escaped and lofted a wobbly, struggling pass into the air. Tyree, running a deep post pattern, pulled up, having already seen his quarterback in trouble.

With Patriots safety Rodney Harrison stuck to him, Tyree had to somehow find a way to catch the ball.

"I just tried to meet the ball at its highest point," Tyree said.

And Tyree, all 6 feet of him, did just that. He ended up with the ball wedged between his hand and his helmet, hanging on for all he was worth.

"I just wasn't letting it go," Tyree said.

Despite getting hammered by Harrison as he fell, Tyree kept possession for a 32-yard gain that parked the Giants 24 yards away from the goal line.

"He made an unbelievable catch, jumping up, holding onto that ball," Manning said.

"That play," Michael Strahan said, "took a couple of years off my life."

Four plays later, Tyree watched Plaxico Burress score the game-winning touchdown. And for Tyree, who caught a touchdown pass himself earlier in the fourth quarter, it was hard to know where to even start on the list of things that made him an improbable Super Bowl star.

There was his spot on the depth chart — he's the Giants fourth wide receiver.

Or that rap he has — even after five years in the league and a Pro Bowl spot in 2005 — that he's "just" a special teams player, not a guy who would be called on in such tight spots.

Or his vertical leap. "Thirty inches maybe," he said. "I may have the worst vertical on the team."

Or the season he just had. It was stunted by everything from injury to personal tragedy — his mother Thelma Tyree, a former Montclair resident, died Dec. 15 at age 59 of a heart attack. Tyree missed the next two games as he mourned

LEFT: David Tyree goes up and makes a miracle catch late in the the second half. *Photo by Andrew Mills*

LEFT: Eli Manning scrambles on third down and avoids a sack to find Tyree in the middle of the field.
Photo by Chris Faytok

ABOVE: Tyree makes a leaping catch, pressing the ball against his helmet, to convert the third down.
Photo by Tim Farrell

his mother.

Or, on a more immediate basis, there was the practice he had on Friday.

"He was dropping every ball," said Amani Toomer, laughing at the memory. "It just goes to show he's a tough guy who makes the catches when they matter."

The touchdown catch in the fourth quarter was certainly one of them. The Giants offense had been held out of the end zone all game before Tyree snagged a little five-yard slant pass from Manning off a play-action fake.

"I had been waiting for that play to be called for the last five weeks," Tyree said. "I'm just glad I caught it."

For the game, Tyree had three catches for 43 yards — and a feel-good Super Bowl for the ages.

"I'm so happy for David," said Tom Quinn, the special teams coach. "It's been a real roller coaster for him and he's really fought through everything. All the years he's put in, to have it culminate in this type of game, it's great."

And, sure, Tyree pointed up to the sky when he caught that touchdown pass. He said he wasn't thinking about his mother in particular when he did it. But he was thinking about her after the game.

And maybe, he realized, he could explain that catch after all.

"I just know she's knocking on the doors of heaven right now, making sure everything is all right for us," Tyree said. "She's always in my heart. I just know she's smiling down on me from heaven." ■

START HERE ☞

ONE FOR THE AGES

Framing the play that turned the Giants from underdogs to world champions.

PHOTO SEQUENCE BY JOHN MUNSON

A look at what is being called the greatest moment in Super Bowl history starts in the upper left-hand corner.

Large photos by Chris Faytok

ABOVE: Amani Toomer makes the catch and stays in bounds. *Photo by John Munson*

RIGHT: Steve Smith makes a key first down catch as Brandon Meriweather makes the hit. *Photo by Chris Faytok*

ABOVE: David Tyree can't watch the final seconds of the game tick away. *Photo by Andrew Mills*

LEFT: Justin Tuck celebrates as time winds down. *Photo by Chris Faytok*

"WE'RE GOING TO SCORE!"

MVP ELI MANNING WRITES AN AMAZING ENDING

By Steve Politi

GLENDALE, Ariz. – His message was short and to the point, and really, none of his teammates needed anything more from Eli Manning. The Giants were 83 yards and one touchdown away from the most improbable victory in Super Bowl history, and the most confident player on the field was leading their huddle.

"We're going to score!" Manning announced, and nobody in that huddle doubted those words. Nobody can ever doubt him now, not after what he did in those next 2½ minutes, writing the most fantastic ending to the wildest postseason run we have ever witnessed.

Eli Manning stole perfection from the New England Patriots. He stole a fourth Super Bowl championship from Tom Brady and Bill Belichick, took it away from

---

LEFT: Eli Manning celebrates the winning touchdown in the final seconds. *Photo by Andrew Mills*

them with a drive for the ages that few could have expected was possible just a few weeks ago.

Broadway Joe? You have company.

"He was walking up and down the sideline, telling everyone, 'This is what we play for. This drive. This moment,'" center Shaun O'Hara said when the 17-14 victory was done. "He never wavered in his confidence, never wavered in his belief that we were going to go down and score."

Manning, the former No. 1 pick who struggled to live up to his name and reputation for much of his career, is now a Super Bowl MVP, just like his big brother was a year ago. But unlike his brother, he had to win three straight playoff games on the road just to get to this stage.

Unlike his brother, he had to face a team in Super Bowl XLII that was looking to complete the greatest season ever. The Patriots were 18-0, their victory parade planned, their perfect season books available for presale. After Manning threw

an incomplete pass on that final drive, defensive tackle Richard Seymour yelled into their huddle, "You guys get ready to go home."

"They had a book out on the Internet," receiver Amani Toomer said. "They were inviting us to their after parties. They tried to rub it in our faces. But we're the more physical team, and they knew that. We came out and punched them in the mouth, and they didn't want it any more."

That final drive started with an 11-yard pass from Manning to Toomer, and the veteran receiver said that's when he knew the Giants were going to score. The rest of the world, the 71,101 at University of Phoenix Stadium and the millions watching on television, needed more evidence.

But they had to believe this victory was possible — maybe even inevitable — a few minutes later. Manning took a snap on third-and-five from the Giants' 44, eluding one pass rusher, then another, somehow scrambling to his right.

"I saw Eli break a tackle," O'Hara said, "which I don't believe he's ever done before in his life."

Manning set his feet and fired a long pass across his body. There was little-used receiver David Tyree, completely covered, somehow grabbing the high throw and attaching it to his helmet like it was covered in Velcro.

He fell backward to the turf, his body bending awkwardly over his defender, but the kid from Montclair — the one who just lost his mother a month and a half ago — managed to hold on to the ball.

Peyton Manning, clapping wildly from the back of a luxury box, said the play would "go down as one of the greatest plays in Super Bowl history."

Michael Strahan, watching from the sideline in disbelief, said, "That play alone took a couple of years off my life."

And Tyree, the receiver who was barely involved in the offense this season? "Some things just don't make sense," he said. "I guess you can put that catch right there on the list."

Four plays later, Manning took a shotgun snap, looked to his left and made the easiest throw he made all game. He found receiver Plaxico Burress in the end zone, and the Giants were 35 seconds away.

Burress was the one who had predicted a 23-17 victory in this game, causing Brady to chuckle that the highest-scoring offense in the league wouldn't crack 20. Who knew Burress was being generous?

"The heart of a champion," Burress said when asked about his quarterback. "Guys were jumping on him, pulling him down by the back of his neck, horse-collaring. Somehow, he managed to break free."

Manning, of course, carried himself no differently after this one than any of his games this season. He was the same quarterback who stood behind the podium and explained that ugly loss to Minnesota, the one with the three interceptions that were returned for touchdowns.

LEFT: Tom Coughlin is doused with water after the win. *Photo by Andrew Mills*

OPPOSITE: The Giants bench explodes after Plaxico Burress catches a touchdown pass in the last minute of the game. *Photo by Tim Farrell*

He was cool and calm, just like he was on the field. "It feels great — just unbelievable," Manning said. "We had no doubt. We believed the whole time, and we made it happen."

Really, he has no idea what is in store for him now. These Giants have just ascended to a unique spot in sports history, joining all-time underdogs such as the U.S. hockey team in 1980, or the Villanova basketball team in 1985, and, yes, Joe Namath and those '69 Jets.

Manning created a moment that will never be forgotten, one that will be replayed again and again. It was a moment nobody thought was possible — except, of course, for the one who orchestrated it.

"We're going to score!" Eli Manning declared, and nobody is going to doubt him any more. ∎

RIGHT: Giants GM Jerry Reese with the Lombardi Trophy.
Photo by Chris Faytok

OPPOSITE: Eli Manning makes his way off the field after the game. *Photo by Chris Faytok*

ABOVE: Brandon Jacobs shares a moment with with fans after the game. *Photo by Chris Faytok*

RIGHT: David Tyree celebrates after the win. *Photo by Chris Faytok*

ABOVE: Michael Strahan embraces defensive coordinator Steve Spagnuolo. *Photo by Andrew Mills*

LEFT: Rich Seubert soaks in the celebration with his son Hunter. *Photo by Chris Faytok*

OPPOSITE: Eli Manning celebrates with David Tyree and Jared Lorenzen as time expires at the end of the game. *Photo by Chris Faytok*

TOP LEFT: Jeff Feagles holds the Lombardi Trophy with Eli Manning. *Photo by Chris Faytok*

BOTTOM LEFT: Michael Strahan celebrates on the podium after the Giants' win.

Photo by Chris Faytok

OPPOSITE: Michael Strahan and Eli Manning play to the crowd during the New York City parade celebrating the Giants' Super Bowl victory over the Patriots.
Photo by John O'Boyle

TOP LEFT: Workers crowd a window overlooking the ticker tape parade up Broadway.
Photo by Andrew Mills

BOTTOM LEFT: Fans try to get close to the players.
Photo by Chris Faytok

TOP RIGHT: The Rev. Dr. James Cooper from Trinity Chuch blesses the Super Bowl champion Giants with incense. *Photo by Chris Faytok*

BOTTOM RIGHT: Fans mob Fred Robbins as he gets off a float to high-five fans along Broadway. *Photo by Chris Faytok*

OPPOSITE: Michael Strahan does the pregame ritual stomp for all the fans at the City Hall rally following the parade down the Canyon of Heroes in Manhattan. *Photo by William Perlman*

RIGHT: David Tyree holds a football to his head as he is introduced at a rally at Giants Stadium, mimicking his spectacular catch. At right is Brandon Jacobs. *Photo by Scott Lituchy*

BELOW: Giants fans cheer as their team comes through the tunnel beneath them during the ceremony at Giants Stadium. *Photo by Tony Kurdzuk*

OPPOSITE: Tom Coughlin carries the Lombardi Trophy around the field after entering the Giants Stadium victory celebration. *Photo by Tony Kurdzuk*

2007-2008 GIANTS GAME STATISTICS

WEEK 1: COWBOYS 45, GIANTS 35

Team	1st	2nd	3rd	4th	Total
Giants	6	10	3	16	35
Cowboys	3	14	14	14	45

1st Quarter

Giants TD: Plaxico Burress 60 yd pass from Eli Manning (failed 2pt Rush), 13:31. Drive: 3 plays, 74 yards in 1:29 New York 6-0

Cowboys FG: Nick Folk 31 yd FG, 6:32. Drive: 14 plays, 67 yards in 6:59 Giants 6-3

2nd Quarter

Giants TD: Marion Barber III 18 yd run (Nick Folk kick), 9:40. Drive: 5 plays, 56 yards in 2:21 Cowboys 10-6

Cowboys TD: Jason Witten 12 yd pass from Tony Romo (Nick Folk kick), 3:59. Drive: 5 plays, 23 yards in 3:45 Cowboys 17-6

Giants TD: Plaxico Burress 4 yd pass from Eli Manning (Lawrence Tynes kick), 0:21. Drive: 12 plays, 75 yards in 3:38 Cowboys 17-13

Giants FG: Lawrence Tynes 44 yd FG, 0:03. Drive: 2 plays, 0 yard in 0:11 Cowboys 17-16

3rd Quarter

Cowboys TD: Terrell Owens 22 yd pass from Tony Romo (Nick Folk kick), 12:00. Drive: 6 plays, 78 yards in 3:00 Cowboys 24-16

Giants FG: Lawrence Tynes 48 yd FG, 5:47. Drive: 11 plays, 48 yards in 6:13 Cowboys 24-19

Cowboys TD: Tony Romo 9 yd run (Nick Folk kick), 1:12. Drive: 4 plays, 67 yards in 1:56 Cowboys 31-19

4th Quarter

Giants FG: Lawrence Tynes 24 yd FG, 13:23. Drive: 6 plays, 53 yards in 2:49 Cowboys 31-22

Cowboys TD: Terrell Owens 47 yd pass from Tony Romo (Nick Folk kick), 11:43. Drive: 3 plays, 71 yards in 1:40 Cowboys 38-22

Giants TD: Derrick Ward 9 yd pass from Eli Manning (failed 2pt Pass from Eli Manning), 7:20. Drive: 9 plays, 80 yards in 4:23 Cowboys 38-28

Giants TD: Plaxico Burress 10 yd pass from Eli Manning (Lawrence Tynes kick), 4:09. Drive: 5 plays, 22 yards in 2:52 Cowboys 38-35

Cowboys TD: Sam Hurd 51 yd pass from Tony Romo (Nick Folk kick), 3:03. Drive: 3 plays, 54 yards in 1:06 Cowboys 45-35

PLAYER STATS: GIANTS

PASSING	CP/AT	YDS	TD	INT
Manning	28/41	312	4	1
Lorenzen	1/3	7	0	0

RUSHING	ATT	YDS	TD	LG
Ward	13	89	0	44
Jacobs	6	26	0	7
Droughns	1	5	0	5
Lorenzen	1	2	0	2
Manning	1	2	0	2

RECEIVING	REC	YDS	TD	LG
Toomer	9	91	0	21
Burress	8	144	3	60
Shockey	5	41	0	14
Ward	4	27	1	10
Smith	3	16	0	7

PLAYER STATS: COWBOYS

PASSING	CP/AT	YDS	TD	INT
Romo	15/24	345	4	1

RUSHING	ATT	YDS	TD	LG
Jones	16	66	0	21
Barber III	11	65	1	19
Romo	3	11	1	9

RECEIVING	REC	YDS	TD	LG
Witten	6	116	1	38
Owens	3	87	2	47
Crayton	3	51	0	25
Hurd	1	51	1	51
Barber III	1	29	0	29
Jones	1	11	0	11

WEEK 2: PACKERS 35, GIANTS 13

Team	1st	2nd	3rd	4th	Total
Giants	0	10	3	0	13
Packers	0	7	7	21	35

2nd Quarter

Packers TD: DeShawn Wynn 6 yd run (Mason Crosby kick), 8:18. Drive: 6 plays, 71 yards in 3:13 Packers 7-0

Giants TD: Plaxico Burress 26 yd pass from Eli Manning (Lawrence Tynes kick), 7:16. Drive: 2 plays, 66 yards in 1:02 Tied 7-7

Giants FG: Lawrence Tynes 48 yd FG, 1:38. Drive: 8 plays, 41 yards in 3:46 Giants 10-7

3rd Quarter

Packers TD: Bubba Franks 2 yd pass from Brett Favre (Mason Crosby kick), 9:07. Drive: 10 plays, 51 yards in 5:53 Packers 14-10

Giants FG: Lawrence Tynes 32 yd FG, 4:22. Drive: 10 plays, 49 yards in 4:45 Packers 14-13

4th Quarter

Packers TD: Donald Lee 3 yd pass from Brett Favre (Mason Crosby kick), 13:33. Drive: 10 plays, 80 yards in 5:49 Packers 21-13

Packers TD: Donald Driver 10 yd pass from Brett Favre (Mason Crosby kick), 11:41. Drive: 5 plays, 22 yards in 1:45 Packers 28-13

Packers TD: DeShawn Wynn 38 yd run (Mason Crosby kick), 4:12. Drive: 5 plays, 53 yards in 2:23 Packers 35-13

PLAYER STATS: GIANTS

PASSING	CP/AT	YDS	TD	INT
Manning	16/29	211	1	1
Wright	1/6	12	0	0
Lorenzen	3/5	21	0	0

RUSHING	ATT	YDS	TD	LG
Ward	15	90	0	26
Moss	1	4	0	4

RECEIVING	REC	YDS	TD	LG
Shockey	5	60	0	19
Ward	4	35	0	12
Mix	3	39	0	21
Toomer	2	48	0	40
Burress	2	32	1	26
Bradshaw	1	11	0	11
Smith	1	10	0	10
Matthews	1	5	0	5
Droughns	1	4	0	4

PLAYER STATS: PACKERS

PASSING	CP/AT	YDS	TD	INT
Favre	29/38	286	3	1

RUSHING	ATT	YDS	TD	LG
Wynn	10	50	2	38
Jackson	17	35	0	8
Favre	2	-2	0	-1

RECEIVING	REC	YDS	TD	LG
Driver	8	73	1	19
Jones	4	75	0	46
Lee	4	35	1	14
Jackson	4	24	0	15
Franks	4	20	1	8
Hall	2	20	0	10
Wynn	2	18	0	10
Grant	1	21	0	21

WEEK 3: GIANTS 24, REDSKINS 17

Team	1st	2nd	3rd	4th	Total
Giants	3	0	7	14	24
Packers	7	10	0	0	17

1st Quarter

Giants FG: Lawrence Tynes 34 yd FG, 7:19. Drive: 9 plays, 54 yards in 3:29 Giants 3-0

Redskins TD: Clinton Portis 1 yd run (Shaun Suisham kick), 4:57. Drive: 2 plays, 6 yards in 0:40 Redskins 7-3

2nd Quarter

Redskins TD: Chris Cooley 8 yd pass from Jason Campbell (Shaun Suisham kick), 7:55. Drive: 7 plays, 72 yards in 4:16 Redskins 14-3

Redskins FG: Shaun Suisham 47 yd FG, 0:00. Drive: 4 plays, 5 yards in 1:33 Redskins 17-3

3rd Quarter

Giants TD: Reuben Droughns 1 yd run (Lawrence Tynes kick), 9:50. Drive: 10 plays, 61 yards in 5:10 Redskins 17-10

4th Quarter

Giants TD: Reuben Droughns 1 yd run (Lawrence Tynes kick), 12:33. Drive: 11 plays, 62 yards in 6:11 Tied 17-17

Giants TD: Plaxico Burress 33 yd pass from Eli Manning (Lawrence Tynes kick), 5:32. Drive: 4 plays, 44 yards in 2:01 Giants 24-17

PLAYER STATS: GIANTS

PASSING	CP/AT	YDS	TD	INT
Manning	21/36	232	1	2

RUSHING	ATT	YDS	TD	LG
Ward	26	94	0	10
Droughns	3	3	2	1
Manning	1	-1	0	-1

RECEIVING	REC	YDS	TD	LG
Ward	6	26	0	10
Burress	5	86	1	33
Shockey	5	79	0	27
Toomer	4	24	0	9
Moss	1	17	0	17

PLAYER STATS: REDSKINS

PASSING	CP/AT	YDS	TD	INT
Campbell	16/34	190	1	0

RUSHING	ATT	YDS	TD	LG
Portis	14	60	1	16
Campbell	4	12	0	10
Betts	7	9	0	13
Moss	1	2	0	2
Randle El	1	-1	0	-1

RECEIVING	REC	YDS	TD	LG
Portis	6	37	0	22
Moss	3	82	0	49
Cooley	3	19	1	8
Randle El	2	32	0	20
Betts	1	13	0	13
Sellers	1	7	0	7

WEEK 4: GIANTS 16, EAGLES 3

Team	1st	2nd	3rd	4th	Total
Giants	0	7	9	0	16
Eagles	0	0	0	3	3

2nd Quarter

Giants TD: Plaxico Burress 9 yd pass from Eli Manning (Lawrence Tynes kick), 11:09. Drive: 4 plays, 49 yards in 1:55 Giants 7-0

3rd Quarter

Giants FG: Lawrence Tynes 29 yd FG, 2:03. Drive: 6 plays, 55 yards in 2:59 Giants 10-0

Giants TD: Kawika Mitchell 17 yd opp fumble return (missed kick), 1:30. Drive: 0 play, 0 yard Giants 16-0

4th Quarter

Eagles FG: David Akers 53 yd FG, 12:51. Drive: 10 plays, 40 yards in 3:39 Giants 16-3

PLAYER STATS: GIANTS

PASSING	CP/AT	YDS	TD	INT
Manning	14/26	135	1	1

RUSHING	ATT	YDS	TD	LG
Ward	19	80	0	15
Droughns	5	8	0	3
Manning	3	-5	0	-1

RECEIVING	REC	YDS	TD	LG
Toomer	4	54	0	19
Burress	4	24	1	10
Ward	3	26	0	10
Shockey	1	17	0	17
Hedgecock	1	9	0	9
Matthews	1	5	0	5

PLAYER STATS: EAGLES

PASSING	CP/AT	YDS	TD	INT
McNabb	15/31	138	0	0

RUSHING	ATT	YDS	TD	LG
Buckhalter	17	103	0	17
Hunt	2	7	0	4
McNabb	4	4	0	2

RECEIVING	REC	YDS	TD	LG
Buckhalter	4	35	0	14
Celek	3	31	0	15
Brown	3	17	0	6
Curtis	2	21	0	12
Avant	1	12	0	12
Schobel	1	11	0	11
Mahe	1	11	0	11

WEEK 5: GIANTS 35, JETS 24

Team	1st	2nd	3rd	4th	Total
Giants	0	7	14	14	35
Jets	7	10	7	0	24

1ST QUARTER

Jets TD: Kerry Rhodes 11 yd opp fumble return (Mike Nugent kick), 8:36. Drive: 0 play, 0 yard Jets 7-0

2nd Quarter

Giants TD: Derrick Ward 8 yd run (Lawrence Tynes kick), 10:54. Drive: 9 plays, 67 yards in 5:29 Tied 7-7

Jets TD: Brad Smith 16 yd pass from Chad Pennington (Mike Nugent kick), 0:33. Drive: 9 plays, 93 yards in 1:46 Jets 14-7

Jets FG: Mike Nugent 47 yd FG, 0:00. Drive: 2 plays, -2 yard in 0:23 Jets 17-7

3rd Quarter

Giants TD: Brandon Jacobs 19 yd run (Lawrence Tynes kick), 11:17. Drive: 6 plays, 80 yards in 3:43 Giants 17-14

Giants TD: Leon Washington 98 yd kick return (Mike Nugent kick), 11:03. Drive: 0 play, 0 yard in 0:14 New York 24-14

Giants TD: Jeremy Shockey 13 yd pass from Eli Manning (Lawrence Tynes kick), 0:33. Drive: 9 plays, 68 yards in 5:06 Giants 24-21

4th Quarter

Giants TD: Plaxico Burress 53 yd pass from Eli Manning (Lawrence Tynes kick), 7:52. Drive: 8 plays, 98 yards in 4:31 Giants 28-24

Giants TD: Aaron Ross 43 yd interception return (Lawrence Tynes kick), 3:15. Drive: 0 play, 0 yard Giants 35-24

PLAYER STATS: GIANTS

PASSING	CP/AT	YDS	TD	INT
Manning	13/25	186	2	1

RUSHING	ATT	YDS	TD	LG
Jacobs	20	100	1	19
Ward	13	56	1	9
Manning	4	17	0	13
Droughns	2	15	0	13

RECEIVING	REC	YDS	TD	LG
Burress	5	124	1	53
Ward	3	8	0	6
Shockey	2	33	1	20
Moss	1	10	0	10
Matthews	1	6	0	6
Hedgecock	1	5	0	5

PLAYER STATS: JETS

PASSING	CP/AT	YDS	TD	INT
Pennington	21/36	229	1	3

RUSHING	ATT	YDS	TD	LG
Jones	13	36	0	7
Washington	9	13	0	10
Pennington	2	6	0	4
Smith	1	0	0	0

RECEIVING	REC	YDS	TD	LG
Coles	8	89	0	28
Cotchery	4	31	0	9
Baker	3	52	0	18
Smith	3	44	1	17
Jones	2	14	0	9
Washington	1	-1	0	-1

WEEK 6: GIANTS 31, FALCONS 10

Team	1st	2nd	3rd	4th	Total
Giants	14	7	0	10	31
Falcons	10	0	0	0	10

1ST QUARTER

Falcons FG: Morten Andersen 47 yd FG, 11:47. Drive: 8 plays, 41 yards in 3:13 Falcons 3-0

Giants TD: Amani Toomer 5 yd pass from Eli Manning (Lawrence Tynes kick), 5:32. Drive: 11 plays, 73 yards in 6:15 Giants 7-3

Falcons TD: Jerious Norwood 67 yd run (Morten Andersen kick), 5:14. Drive: 1 play, 67 yards in 0:18 Falcons 10-7

Giants TD: Reuben Droughns 1 yd run (Lawrence Tynes kick), 2:13. Drive: 6 plays, 82 yards in 3:01 Giants 14-10

2nd Quarter

Giants TD: Plaxico Burress 43 yd pass from Eli Manning (Lawrence Tynes kick), 8:21. Drive: 4 plays, 62 yards in 2:22 Giants 21-10

4th Quarter

Giants FG: Lawrence Tynes 32 yd FG, 10:52. Drive: 13 plays, 79 yards in 7:57 Giants 24-10

Giants TD: Derrick Ward 9 yd run (Lawrence Tynes kick), 3:08. Drive: 4 plays, 67 yards in 1:42 Giants 31-10

PLAYER STATS: GIANTS

PASSING	CP/AT	YDS	TD	INT
Manning	27/39	303	2	2

RUSHING	ATT	YDS	TD	LG
Droughns	14	90	1	45
Jacobs	13	86	0	20
Ward	8	12	1	9

RECEIVING	REC	YDS	TD	LG
Toomer	7	89	1	17
Burress	6	97	1	43
Shockey	5	63	0	21
Moss	4	19	0	7
Hedgecock	2	17	0	9
Ward	2	16	0	9
Jacobs	1	2	0	2

PLAYER STATS: FALCONS

PASSING	CP/AT	YDS	TD	INT
Harrington	18/39	209	0	1

RUSHING	ATT	YDS	TD	LG
Norwood	6	87	1	67
Dunn	8	15	0	6
Harrington	1	1	0	1

RECEIVING	REC	YDS	TD	LG
White	4	64	0	38
Norwood	4	51	0	21
Horn	2	25	0	14
Jenkins	2	23	0	18
Dunn	2	13	0	11
Milner	1	15	0	15
Crumpler	1	9	0	9
Robinson	1	8	0	8
Mughelli	1	1	0	1

WEEK 7: GIANTS 33, 49ERS 15

Team	1st	2nd	3rd	4th	Total
Giants	6	13	7	7	33
49ers	0	7	2	6	15

1ST QUARTER

Giants TD: Amani Toomer 4 yd pass from Eli Manning (missed kick), 7:47. Drive: 13 plays, 83 yards in 7:13 Giants 6-0

2nd Quarter

49ers TD: Arnaz Battle 17 yd pass from Trent Dilfer (Joe Nedney kick), 9:50. Drive: 11 plays, 81 yards in 6:25 49ers 7-6

Giants TD: Brandon Jacobs 5 yd run (Lawrence Tynes kick), 6:15. Drive: 4 plays, 27 yards in 1:12 Giants 13-7

Giants FG: Lawrence Tynes 29 yd FG, 2:50. Drive: 6 plays, 19 yards in 3:09 Giants 16-7

Giants FG: Lawrence Tynes 39 yd FG, 0:17. Drive: 9 plays, 68 yards in 1:18 Giants 19-7

3rd Quarter

Giants TD: Osi Umenyiora 75 yd opp fumble return (Lawrence Tynes kick), 12:53. Drive: 0 play, 0 yard Giants 26-7

49ers SAF: Team safety, 8:51. Drive: Giants 26-9

4th Quarter

Giants TD: Jeremy Shockey 2 yd pass from Eli Manning (Lawrence Tynes kick), 10:50. Drive: 4 plays, 5 yards in 2:25 Giants 33-9

49ers TD: Darrell Jackson 1 yd pass from Trent Dilfer (failed 2pt Pass from Trent Dilfer), 0:16. Drive: 10 plays, 53 yards in 3:00 Giants 33-15

PLAYER STATS: GIANTS

PASSING	CP/AT	YDS	TD	INT
Manning	18/31	146	2	1
Wright	0/1	0	0	0

RUSHING	ATT	YDS	TD	LG
Jacobs	18	107	1	12
Ward	7	27	0	11
Droughns	5	7	0	4
Wright	1	-1	0	-1

RECEIVING	REC	YDS	TD	LG
Burress	5	43	0	18
Shockey	5	39	1	14
Toomer	3	36	1	24
Jacobs	3	16	0	9
Ward	2	12	0	6

PLAYER STATS: 49ERS

PASSING	CP/AT	YDS	TD	INT
Dilfer	23/38	209	2	2

RUSHING	ATT	YDS	TD	LG
Gore	14	88	0	24
Dilfer	3	11	0	11
Robinson	1	4	0	4

RECEIVING	REC	YDS	TD	LG
Battle	6	57	1	17
Davis	4	22	0	7
Gore	3	23	0	12
Lelie	2	52	0	47
Robinson	2	13	0	11
Hicks	2	12	0	9
Jackson	2	6	1	5
Gilmore	1	20	0	20
Walker	1	4	0	4

WEEK 8: GIANTS 13, DOLPHINS 10

Team	1st	2nd	3rd	4th	Total
Giants	3	10	0	0	13
Dolphins	0	0	3	7	10

1st Quarter

Giants FG: Lawrence Tynes 20 yd FG, 3:33. Drive: 11 plays, 59 yards in 4:47 Giants 3-0

2nd Quarter

Giants TD: Eli Manning 10 yd run (Lawrence Tynes kick), 0:59. Drive: 14 plays, 69 yards in 8:07 Giants 10-0

Giants FG: Lawrence Tynes 41 yd FG, 0:02. Drive: 4 plays, 11 yards in 0:24 Giants 13-0

3rd Quarter

Dolphins FG: Jay Feely 29 yd FG, 1:04. Drive: 8 plays, 40 yards in 4:12 Giants 13-3

4th Quarter

Dolphins TD: Ted Ginn Jr. 21 yd pass from Cleo Lemon (Jay Feely kick), 1:54. Drive: 12 plays, 80 yards in 2:11 Giants 13-10

PLAYER STATS: GIANTS

PASSING	CP/AT	YDS	TD	INT
Manning	8/22	59	0	0

RUSHING	ATT	YDS	TD	LG
Jacobs	23	131	0	15
Droughns	8	27	0	8
Manning	5	25	1	18
Shockey	1	6	0	6

RECEIVING	REC	YDS	TD	LG
Shockey	3	26	0	21
Burress	2	14	0	9
Jacobs	2	6	0	6
Toomer	1	13	0	13

PLAYER STATS: DOLPHINS

PASSING	CP/AT	YDS	TD	INT
Lemon	17/30	149	1	0

RUSHING	ATT	YDS	TD	LG
Chatman	16	79	0	22
Lemon	5	28	0	11
Cobbs	4	19	0	6
Booker	1	0	0	0

RECEIVING	REC	YDS	TD	LG
Peelle	6	42	0	10
Booker	3	31	0	13
Chatman	3	21	0	9
Hagan	2	27	0	15
Ginn Jr.	1	21	1	21
Halterman	1	7	0	7
Mauia	1	0	0	0

WEEK 9: BYE

WEEK 10: COWBOYS 31, GIANTS 20

Team	1st	2nd	3rd	4th	Total
Giants	7	10	0	3	20
Cowboys	7	10	7	7	31

1st Quarter

Cowboys TD: Tony Curtis 15 yd pass from Tony Romo (Nick Folk kick), 11:10. Drive: 7 plays, 65 yards in 3:50 Cowboys 7-0

Giants TD: Jeremy Shockey 8 yd pass from Eli Manning (Lawrence Tynes kick), 6:13. Drive: 8 plays, 67 yards in 4:57 Tied 7-7

2nd Quarter

Cowboys FG: Nick Folk 44 yd FG, 14:56. Drive: 6 plays, 13 yards in 2:56 Cowboys 10-7

Giants TD: Reuben Droughns 1 yd run (Lawrence Tynes kick), 4:33. Drive: 11 plays, 60 yards in 7:22 Giants 14-10

Cowboys TD: Patrick Crayton 20 yd pass from Tony Romo (Nick Folk kick), 0:27. Drive: 7 plays, 68 yards in 1:21 Cowboys 17-14

Giants FG: Lawrence Tynes 40 yd FG, 0:01. Drive: 2 plays, 44 yards in 0:26 Tied 17-17

3rd Quarter

Cowboys TD: Terrell Owens 25 yd pass from Tony Romo (Nick Folk kick), 7:14. Drive: 12 plays, 86 yards in 6:27 Cowboys 24-17

4th Quarter

Giants FG: Lawrence Tynes 26 yd FG, 13:18. Drive: 16 plays, 75 yards in 8:56 Cowboys 24-20

Cowboys TD: Terrell Owens 50 yd pass from Tony Romo (Nick Folk kick), 10:43. Drive: 5 plays, 70 yards in 2:35 Cowboys 31-20

PLAYER STATS: GIANTS

PASSING	CP/AT	YDS	TD	INT
Manning	23/34	236	1	2

RUSHING	ATT	YDS	TD	LG
Jacobs	24	95	0	16
Droughns	3	8	1	5
Manning	1	3	0	3

RECEIVING	REC	YDS	TD	LG
Shockey	12	129	1	29
Burress	4	24	0	11
Toomer	3	37	0	23
Boss	1	18	0	18
Moss	1	13	0	13
Jacobs	1	10	0	10
Droughns	1	5	0	5

PLAYER STATS: COWBOYS

PASSING	CP/AT	YDS	TD	INT
Romo	20/28	247	4	1

RUSHING	ATT	YDS	TD	LG
Jones	11	48	0	20
Barber	12	34	0	6
Romo	2	-2	0	0

RECEIVING	REC	YDS	TD	LG
Owens	6	125	2	50
Crayton	5	66	1	20
Barber	3	-1	0	5
Hurd	2	21	0	12
Witten	2	12	0	8
Curtis	1	15	1	15
Fasano	1	9	0	9

WEEK 11: GIANTS 16, LIONS 10

Team	1st	2nd	3rd	4th	Total
Giants	3	7	3	3	16
Lions	0	0	3	7	10

1st Quarter

Giants FG: Lawrence Tynes 28 yd FG, 0:37. Drive: 10 plays, 81 yards in 5:11 Giants 3-0

2nd Quarter

Giants TD: Brandon Jacobs 10 yd pass from Eli Manning (Lawrence Tynes kick), 0:23. Drive: 11 plays, 80 yards in 3:44 Giants 10-0

3rd Quarter

Lions FG: Jason Hanson 42 yd FG, 10:52. Drive: 8 plays, 43 yards in 3:40 Giants 10-3

Giants FG: Lawrence Tynes 46 yd FG, 2:39. Drive: 6 plays, 30 yards in 3:18 Giants 13-3

4th Quarter

Giants FG: Lawrence Tynes 20 yd FG, 11:15. Drive: 9 plays, 53 yards in 4:50 Giants 16-3

Lions TD: Calvin Johnson 35 yd pass from Jon Kitna (Jason Hanson kick), 4:34. Drive: 4 plays, 82 yards in 1:18 Giants 16-10

PLAYER STATS: GIANTS

PASSING	CP/AT	YDS	TD	INT
Manning	28/39	283	1	0

RUSHING	ATT	YDS	TD	LG
Jacobs	11	54	0	18
Droughns	11	13	0	7
Manning	5	5	0	9

RECEIVING	REC	YDS	TD	LG
Shockey	5	41	0	12
Jacobs	4	49	1	34
Burress	4	47	0	18
Moss	4	46	0	14
Toomer	4	39	0	17
Droughns	3	26	0	11
Hedgecock	2	14	0	9
Boss	1	15	0	15
Matthews	1	6	0	6

PLAYER STATS: LIONS

PASSING	CP/AT	YDS	TD	INT
Kitna	28/43	377	1	3

RUSHING	ATT	YDS	TD	LG
Jones	11	25	0	8

RECEIVING	REC	YDS	TD	LG
McDonald	7	113	0	32
Williams	6	106	0	28
Furrey	5	41	0	18
Johnson	3	45	1	35
Jones	3	12	0	7
FitzSimmons	1	21	0	21
Walters	1	19	0	19
McHugh	1	18	0	18
Bradley	1	2	0	2

WEEK 12: VIKINGS 41, GIANTS 17

Team	1st	2nd	3rd	4th	Total
Giants	7	0	3	7	17
Vikings	14	10	3	14	41

1st Quarter

Vikings TD: Sidney Rice 60 yd pass from Tarvaris Jackson (Ryan Longwell kick), 14:19. Drive: 2 plays, 60 yards in 0:41 Vikings 7-0

Giants TD: Reuben Droughns 1 yd run (Lawrence Tynes kick), 9:25. Drive: 8 plays, 65 yards in 4:54 Tied 7-7

Vikings TD: Darren Sharper 20 yd interception return (Ryan Longwell kick), 3:15. Drive: 0 play, 0 yard Vikings 14-7

2nd Quarter

Vikings TD: Chester Taylor 8 yd run (Ryan Longwell kick), 9:49. Drive: 1 play, 8 yards in 0:09 Vikings 21-7

Vikings FG: Ryan Longwell 46 yd FG, 3:16. Drive: 9 plays, 37 yards in 4:47 Vikings 24-7

3rd Quarter

Giants FG: Lawrence Tynes 48 yd FG, 11:07. Drive: 10 plays, 48 yards in 3:53 Vikings 24-10

Vikings FG: Ryan Longwell 26 yd FG, 1:43. Drive: 14 plays, 69 yards in 9:24 Vikings 27-10

4th Quarter

Vikings TD: Dwight Smith 93 yd interception return (Ryan Longwell kick), 13:41. Drive: 0 play, 0 yard Vikings 34-10

Vikings TD: Chad Greenway 37 yd interception return (Ryan Longwell kick), 12:59. Drive: 0 play, 0 yard Vikings 41-10

Giants TD: Plaxico Burress 6 yd pass from Eli Manning (Lawrence Tynes kick), 5:54. Drive: 7 plays, 44 yards in 2:51 Vikings 41-17

PLAYER STATS: GIANTS

PASSING	CP/AT	YDS	TD	INT
Manning	21/49	273	1	4

RUSHING	ATT	YDS	TD	LG
Droughns	15	46	1	10
Bradshaw	4	29	0	11

RECEIVING	REC	YDS	TD	LG
Burress	7	93	1	32
Toomer	4	83	0	31
Shockey	4	44	0	20
Moss	3	39	0	20
Droughns	1	6	0	6
Hixon	1	5	0	5
Matthews	1	3	0	3

PLAYER STATS: VIKINGS

PASSING	CP/AT	YDS	TD	INT
Jackson	10/12	129	1	0

RUSHING	ATT	YDS	TD	LG
Taylor	31	77	1	13
Jackson	5	38	0	19
Moore	3	12	0	8

RECEIVING	REC	YDS	TD	LG
Rice	3	82	1	60
Wade	2	14	0	9
Taylor	2	12	0	11
Shiancoe	1	13	0	13
Williamson	1	8	0	8
Dugan	1	0	0	0

WEEK 13: GIANTS 21, BEARS 16

Team	1st	2nd	3rd	4th	Total
Giants	0	7	0	14	21
Bears	7	6	3	0	16

1st Quarter

Bears TD: Desmond Clark 1 yd pass from Rex Grossman (Robbie Gould kick), 9:58. Drive: 9 plays, 79 yards in 3:08 Bears 7-0

2nd Quarter

Giants TD: Derrick Ward 2 yd run (Lawrence Tynes kick), 10:25. Drive: 4 plays, 32 yards in 1:40 Tied 7-7

Bears FG: Robbie Gould 35 yd FG, 4:38. Drive: 8 plays, 54 yards in 3:13 Bears 10-7

Bears FG: Robbie Gould 46 yd FG, 0:00. Drive: 14 plays, 62 yards in 2:53 Bears 13-7

3rd Quarter

Bears FG: Robbie Gould 41 yd FG, 10:52. Drive: 7 plays, 2 yards in 3:04 Bears 16-7

4th Quarter

Giants TD: Amani Toomer 6 yd pass from Eli Manning (Lawrence Tynes kick), 6:54. Drive: 11 plays, 75 yards in 4:51 Bears 16-14

Giants TD: Reuben Droughns 2 yd run (Lawrence Tynes kick), 1:33. Drive: 9 plays, 77 yards in 3:22 Giants 21-16

PLAYER STATS: GIANTS

PASSING	CP/AT	YDS	TD	INT
Manning	16/27	195	1	2

RUSHING	ATT	YDS	TD	LG
Ward	24	154	1	33
Droughns	10	25	1	9
Bradshaw	1	2	0	2
Manning	1	2	0	2
Hixon	1	-8	0	-8

RECEIVING	REC	YDS	TD	LG
Toomer	6	69	1	18
Burress	3	36	0	15
Tyree	2	32	0	24
Ward	2	29	0	17
Shockey	2	25	0	18
Boss	1	4	0	4

PLAYER STATS: BEARS

PASSING	CP/AT	YDS	TD	INT
Grossman	25/46	296	1	0

RUSHING	ATT	YDS	TD	LG
Peterson	22	67	0	9
Hester	1	1	0	1

RECEIVING	REC	YDS	TD	LG
Peterson	7	82	0	29
Clark	5	76	1	44
Berrian	3	59	0	50
Muhammad	3	52	0	21
Davis	2	17	0	12
Olsen	2	7	0	4
Bradley	1	7	0	7
McKie	1	0	0	0
Hester	1	-4	0	-4

WEEK 14: GIANTS 16, EAGLES 13

Team	1st	2nd	3rd	4th	Total
Giants	0	6	10	0	16
Eagles	7	0	3	3	13

1st Quarter

Eagles TD: Brian Westbrook 18 yd pass from Donovan McNabb (David Akers kick), 11:47.Drive: 6 plays, 68 yards in 3:13 Eagles 7-0

2nd Quarter

Giants FG: Lawrence Tynes 19 yd FG, 11:06. Drive: 13 plays, 84 yards in 6:25 Eagles 7-3

Giants FG: Lawrence Tynes 23 yd FG, 0:00. Drive: 9 plays, 45 yards in 1:23 Eagles 7-6

3rd Quarter

Eagles FG: David Akers 29 yd FG, 12:42. Drive: 4 plays, -4 yard in 1:20 Eagles 10-6

Giants TD: Plaxico Burress 20 yd pass from Eli Manning (Lawrence Tynes kick), 5:59. Drive: 3 plays, 37 yards in 1:11 Giants 13-10

Giants FG: Lawrence Tynes 23 yd FG, 0:48. Drive: 7 plays, 61 yards in 3:06 Giants 16-10

4th Quarter

Eagles FG: David Akers 39 yd FG, 8:26. Drive: 12 plays, 57 yards in 7:22 Giants 16-13

PLAYER STATS: GIANTS

PASSING	CP/AT	YDS	TD	INT
Manning	17/31	219	1	0

RUSHING	ATT	YDS	TD	LG
Jacobs	22	70	0	21
Droughns	3	34	0	35
Manning	2	7	0	8

RECEIVING	REC	YDS	TD	LG
Burress	7	136	1	41
Toomer	3	37	0	19
Jacobs	3	11	0	11
Moss	2	28	0	17
Shockey	1	4	0	4
Matthews	1	3	0	3

PLAYER STATS: EAGLES

PASSING	CP/AT	YDS	TD	INT
McNabb	20/30	179	1	0
Lewis	0/1	0	0	0

RUSHING	ATT	YDS	TD	LG
Westbrook	20	116	0	21
McNabb	4	11	0	5
Buckhalter	2	9	0	5
Brown	1	5	0	5
Tapeh	1	0	0	0

RECEIVING	REC	YDS	TD	LG
Brown	7	71	0	19
Westbrook	5	38	1	18
Curtis	3	26	0	13
Lewis	1	18	0	18
Schobel	1	9	0	9
Smith	1	8	0	8
Avant	1	5	0	5
Tapeh	1	4	0	4

WEEK 15: REDSKINS 22, GIANTS 10

Team	1st	2nd	3rd	4th	Total
Giants	0	3	7	0	10
Redskins	3	13	6	0	22

1st Quarter

Redskins FG: Shaun Suisham 50 yd FG, 2:23. Drive: 6 plays, 20 yards in 2:24 Redskins 3-0

2nd Quarter

Redskins FG: Shaun Suisham 31 yd FG, 10:12. Drive: 6 plays, 67 yards in 2:40 Redskins 6-0

Redskins TD: Ladell Betts 14 yd run (Shaun Suisham kick), 3:07. Drive: 6 plays, 50 yards in 2:05 Redskins 13-0

Giants FG: Lawrence Tynes 35 yd FG, 1:16. Drive: 8 plays, 55 yards in 1:51 Redskins 13-3

Redskins FG: Shaun Suisham 28 yd FG, 0:00. Drive: 7 plays, 62 yards in 1:16 Redskins 16-3

3rd Quarter

Redskins TD: Clinton Portis 5 yd run (failed 2pt Pass from Todd Collins), 12:08. Drive: 5 plays, 46 yards in 2:52 Redskins 22-3

Giants TD: Kevin Boss 19 yd pass from Eli Manning (Lawrence Tynes kick), 4:37. Drive: 6 plays, 48 yards in 2:24 Redskins 22-10

PLAYER STATS: GIANTS

PASSING	CP/AT	YDS	TD	INT
Manning	18/53	184	1	0

RUSHING	ATT	YDS	TD	LG
Jacobs	25	130	0	18
Bradshaw	1	8	0	8
Manning	1	1	0	1
Droughns	1	0	0	0

RECEIVING	REC	YDS	TD	LG
Moss	5	53	0	15
Burress	3	35	0	18
Jacobs	3	30	0	11
Boss	2	31	1	19
Shockey	2	18	0	15
Droughns	1	8	0	8
Smith	1	8	0	8
Bradshaw	1	1	0	1

PLAYER STATS: REDSKINS

PASSING	CP/AT	YDS	TD	INT
Collins	8/25	166	0	0

RUSHING	ATT	YDS	TD	LG
Portis	25	126	1	31
Betts	8	29	1	14
Collins	2	-2	0	-1

RECEIVING	REC	YDS	TD	LG
Moss	3	75	0	36
Cooley	2	34	0	19
Yoder	1	30	0	30
Sellers	1	19	0	19
Betts	1	8	0	8

WEEK 16: GIANTS 38, BILLS 21

Team	1st	2nd	3rd	4th	Total
Giants	0	17	0	21	38
Bills	14	0	7	0	21

1st Quarter

Bills TD: Michael Gaines 3 yd pass from Trent Edwards (Rian Lindell kick), 10:24. Drive: 7 plays, 60 yards in 4:36 Bills 7-0

Bills TD: Lee Evans 4 yd pass from Trent Edwards (Rian Lindell kick), 5:31. Drive: 6 plays, 66 yards in 3:01 Bills 14-0

2nd Quarter

Giants TD: Brandon Jacobs 6 yd run (Lawrence Tynes kick), 11:38. Drive: 5 plays, 23 yards in 1:58 Bills 14-7

Giants TD: Brandon Jacobs 43 yd run (Lawrence Tynes kick), 8:32. Drive: 4 plays, 57 yards in 1:47 Tied 14-14

Giants FG: Lawrence Tynes 42 yd FG, 2:35. Drive: 7 plays, 32 yards in 4:16 Giants 17-14

3rd Quarter

Bills TD: Marshawn Lynch 3 yd run (Rian Lindell kick), 13:54. Drive: 2 plays, 31 yards in 0:51 Bills 21-17

4th Quarter

Giants TD: Kawika Mitchell 20 yd interception return (Lawrence Tynes kick), 14:05. Drive: 0 play, 0 yard Giants 24-21

Giants TD: Ahmad Bradshaw 88 yd run (Lawrence Tynes kick), 6:12. Drive: 1 play, 88 yards in 0:15 Giants 31-21

Giants TD: Corey Webster 34 yd interception return (Lawrence Tynes kick), 5:50. Drive: 0 play, 0 yard Giants 38-21

PLAYER STATS: GIANTS

PASSING	CP/AT	YDS	TD	INT
Manning	7/15	111	0	2

RUSHING	ATT	YDS	TD	LG
Bradshaw	17	151	1	88
Jacobs	25	143	2	43
Manning	2	0	0	0
Droughns	3	-5	0	0

RECEIVING	REC	YDS	TD	LG
Toomer	5	99	0	39
Jacobs	1	6	0	6
Burress	1	6	0	6

PLAYER STATS: BILLS

PASSING	CP/AT	YDS	TD	INT
Edwards	9/26	161	2	3

RUSHING	ATT	YDS	TD	LG
Lynch	18	70	1	28
Jackson	6	37	0	19
Edwards	2	7	0	8
Wright	1	3	0	3
Moorman	1	0	0	0

RECEIVING	REC	YDS	TD	LG
Evans	3	43	1	21
Lynch	2	42	0	30
Gaines	2	23	1	20
Parrish	1	42	0	42
Reed	1	11	0	11

WEEK 17: PATRIOTS 38, GIANTS 35

Team	1st	2nd	3rd	4th	Total
Giants	7	14	7	7	35
Patriots	7	13	7	15	38

1st Quarter

Giants TD: Brandon Jacobs 7 yd pass from Eli Manning (Lawrence Tynes kick), 10:59. Drive: 7 plays, 74 yards in 4:01 Giants 7-0

Patriots FG: Stephen Gostkowski 37 yd FG, 5:19. Drive: 12 plays, 54 yards in 5:40 Giants 7-3

2nd Quarter

Patriots TD: Randy Moss 4 yd pass from Tom Brady (Stephen Gostkowski kick), 14:55. Drive: 8 plays, 50 yards in 3:41 Patriots 10-7

Giants TD: Domenik Hixon 74 yd kick return (Lawrence Tynes kick), 14:44. Drive: 0 play, 0 yard in 0:11 Giants 14-10

Patriots FG: Stephen Gostkowski 45 yd FG, 9:59. Drive: 8 plays, 39 yards in 4:45 Giants 14-13

Patriots FG: Stephen Gostkowski 37 yd FG, 1:59. Drive: 11 plays, 61 yards in 5:41 Patriots 16-14

Giants TD: Kevin Boss 3 yd pass from Eli Manning (Lawrence Tynes kick), 0:13. Drive: 8 plays, 85 yards in 1:46 Giants 21-16

3rd Quarter

Giants TD: Plaxico Burress 19 yd pass from Eli Manning (Lawrence Tynes kick), 9:12. Drive: 7 plays, 60 yards in 4:10 Giants 28-16

Patriots TD: Laurence Maroney 6 yd run (Stephen Gostkowski kick), 4:00. Drive: 8 plays, 73 yards in 5:12 Giants 28-23

4th Quarter

Patriots TD: Randy Moss 65 yd pass from Tom Brady (Laurence Maroney 2pt Rush), 11:06. Drive: 3 plays, 65 yards in 0:23 Patriots 31-28

Patriots TD: Laurence Maroney 5 yd run (Stephen Gostkowski kick), 4:36. Drive: 9 plays, 52 yards in 5:17 Patriots 38-28

Giants TD: Plaxico Burress 3 yd pass from Eli Manning (Lawrence Tynes kick), 1:04. Drive: 11 plays, 68 yards in 3:32 Patriots 38-35

PLAYER STATS: GIANTS

PASSING	CP/AT	YDS	TD	INT
Manning	22/32	251	4	1

RUSHING	ATT	YDS	TD	LG
Jacobs	15	67	0	16
Manning	3	13	0	11
Droughns	1	-1	0	-1

RECEIVING	REC	YDS	TD	LG
Jacobs	5	44	1	17
Burress	4	84	2	52
Boss	4	50	1	23
Toomer	4	41	0	19
Smith	3	29	0	12
Tyree	2	3	0	4

PLAYER STATS: PATRIOTS

PASSING	CP/AT	YDS	TD	INT
Brady	32/42	356	2	0

RUSHING	ATT	YDS	TD	LG
Maroney	19	46	2	13
Evans	1	4	0	4
Faulk	2	-2	0	0
Brady	4	-4	0	-1

RECEIVING	REC	YDS	TD	LG
Welker	11	122	0	28
Faulk	8	64	0	13
Moss	6	100	2	65
Watson	4	38	0	21
Stallworth	3	32	0	17

WEEK 18: GIANTS 24, BUCCANEERS 14

Team	1st	2nd	3rd	4th	Total
Giants	0	14	3	7	24
Buccaneers	7	0	0	7	14

1st Quarter

Bucs TD: Earnest Graham 1 yd run (Matt Bryant kick), 1:49. Drive: 10 plays, 54 yards in 5:13 Bucs 7-0

2nd Quarter

Giants TD: Brandon Jacobs 5 yd pass from Eli Manning (Lawrence Tynes kick), 10:02. Drive: 8 plays, 53 yards in 4:04 Tied 7-7

Giants TD: Brandon Jacobs 8 yd run (Lawrence Tynes kick), 4:06. Drive: 7 plays, 65 yards in 4:23 Giants 14-7

3rd Quarter

Giants FG: Lawrence Tynes 25 yd FG, 9:56. Drive: 9 plays, 23 yards in 4:54 Giants 17-7

4th Quarter

Giants TD: Amani Toomer 4 yd pass from Eli Manning (Lawrence Tynes kick), 8:03. Drive: 15 plays, 92 yards in 8:37 Giants 24-7

Bucs TD: Alex Smith 6 yd pass from Jeff Garcia (Matt Bryant kick), 3:25. Drive: 12 plays, 88 yards in 4:38 Giants 24-14

PLAYER STATS: GIANTS

PASSING	CP/AT	YDS	TD	INT
Manning	20/27	185	2	0

RUSHING	ATT	YDS	TD	LG
Bradshaw	17	66	0	8
Jacobs	13	34	1	9

RECEIVING	REC	YDS	TD	LG
Toomer	7	74	1	17
Burress	4	38	0	14
Smith	3	29	0	21
Jacobs	2	16	1	11
Boss	2	14	0	11
Bradshaw	1	9	0	9
Hedgecock	1	5	0	5

PLAYER STATS: BUCCANEERS

PASSING	CP/AT	YDS	TD	INT
Garcia	23/39	207	1	2

RUSHING	ATT	YDS	TD	LG
Graham	18	63	1	11
Pittman	1	5	0	5
Askew	1	3	0	3
Garcia	1	2	0	2
Galloway	1	-4	0	-4

RECEIVING	REC	YDS	TD	LG
Pittman	5	62	0	26
Hilliard	4	27	0	9
Graham	4	27	0	14
Clayton	3	39	0	15
Smith	3	26	1	15
Askew	2	12	0	7
Galloway	1	9	0	9
Stevens	1	5	0	5

WEEK 19: GIANTS 21, COWBOYS 17

Team	1st	2nd	3rd	4th	Total
Giants	7	7	0	7	21
Cowboys	0	14	3	0	17

1st Quarter

Giants TD: Amani Toomer 52 yd pass from Eli Manning (Lawrence Tynes kick), 11:50. Drive: 6 plays, 77 yards in 3:10 Giants 7-0

2nd Quarter

Cowboys TD: Terrell Owens 5 yd pass from Tony Romo (Nick Folk kick), 14:56. Drive: 9 plays, 96 yards in 4:57 Tied 7-7

Cowboys TD: Marion Barber 1 yd run (Nick Folk kick), 0:53. Drive: 20 plays, 90 yards in 10:28 Cowboys 14-7

Giants TD: Amani Toomer 4 yd pass from Eli Manning (Lawrence Tynes kick), 0:07. Drive: 7 plays, 71 yards in 0:46 Tied 14-14

3rd Quarter

Cowboys FG: Nick Folk 34 yd FG, 6:53. Drive: 14 plays, 62 yards in 8:07 Cowboys 17-14

4th Quarter

Giants TD: Brandon Jacobs 1 yd run (Lawrence Tynes kick), 13:29. Drive: 6 plays, 37 yards in 2:24 Giants 21-17

PLAYER STATS: GIANTS

PASSING	CP/AT	YDS	TD	INT
Manning	12/18	163	2	0

RUSHING	ATT	YDS	TD	LG
Jacobs	14	54	1	10
Bradshaw	6	34	0	11

Manning	3	2	0	2

RECEIVING	REC	YDS	TD	LG
Toomer	4	80	2	52
Smith	4	48	0	22
Boss	1	19	0	19
Bradshaw	1	6	0	6
Jacobs	1	5	0	5
Burress	1	5	0	5

PLAYER STATS: COWBOYS

PASSING	CP/AT	YDS	TD	INT
Romo	18/36	201	1	1

RUSHING	ATT	YDS	TD	LG
Barber	27	129	1	36
Romo	3	17	0	11
Jones	3	8	0	4

RECEIVING	REC	YDS	TD	LG
Witten	7	81	0	20
Owens	4	49	1	20
Crayton	3	27	0	16
Glenn	2	30	0	19
Barber	1	9	0	9
Fasano	1	5	0	5

WEEK 20: GIANTS 23, PACKERS 20

Team	1st	2nd	3rd	4th	OT	Total
Giants	3	3	14	0	3	21
Packers	0	10	7	3	0	17

1st Quarter

Giants FG: Lawrence Tynes 29 yd FG, 4:50. Drive: 14 plays, 71 yards in 7:48 Giants 3-0

2nd Quarter

Giants FG: Lawrence Tynes 37 yd FG, 11:41. Drive: 7 plays, 38 yards in 3:04 Giants 6-0

Packers TD: Donald Driver 90 yd pass from Brett Favre (Mason Crosby kick), 11:18. Drive: 1 play, 90 yards in 0:23 Packers 7-6

Packers FG: Mason Crosby 36 yd FG, 1:30. Drive: 8 plays, 29 yards in 2:58 Packers 10-6

3rd Quarter

Giants TD: Brandon Jacobs 1 yd run (Lawrence Tynes kick), 7:56. Drive: 12 plays, 69 yards in 7:04 Giants 13-10

Packers TD: Donald Lee 12 yd pass from Brett Favre (Mason Crosby kick), 5:00. Drive: 6 plays, 39 yards in 2:56 Packers 17-13

Giants TD: Ahmad Bradshaw 4 yd run (Lawrence Tynes kick), 2:12. Drive: 7 plays, 57 yards in 2:48 Giants 20-17

4th Quarter

Packers FG: Mason Crosby 37 yd FG, 11:46. Drive: 4 plays, 0 yard in 2:14 Tied 20-20

Overtime

Giants FG: Lawrence Tynes 47 yd FG, 12:25. Drive: 4 plays, 5 yards in 1:39 Giants 23-20

PLAYER STATS: GIANTS

PASSING	CP/AT	YDS	TD	INT
Manning	21/40	251	0	0

RUSHING	ATT	YDS	TD	LG
Jacobs	21	67	1	12
Bradshaw	16	63	1	10
Manning	2	4	0	2

RECEIVING	REC	YDS	TD	LG
Burress	11	151	0	32
Toomer	4	42	0	23
Smith	2	25	0	14
Boss	1	12	0	12
Bradshaw	1	9	0	9
Jacobs	1	8	0	8
Tyree	1	4	0	4

PLAYER STATS: PACKERS

PASSING	CP/AT	YDS	TD	INT
Favre	19/35	236	2	2

RUSHING	ATT	YDS	TD	LG
Grant	13	29	0	13
Favre	1	-1	0	-1

RECEIVING	REC	YDS	TD	LG
Driver	5	141	1	90
Robinson	4	16	0	16
Lee	3	35	1	18
Morency	2	9	0	7
Jennings	1	14	0	14
Hall	1	12	0	12
Franks	1	11	0	11
Jackson	1	1	0	1
Grant	1	-3	0	-3

SUPER BOWL: GIANTS 17, PATRIOTS 14

Team	1st	2nd	3rd	4th	Total
Giants	3	0	0	14	17
Patriots	0	7	0	7	14

1st Quarter

Giants FG: Lawrence Tynes 32 yd FG, 5:01. Drive: 16 plays, 63 yards in 9:59 Giants 3-0

2nd Quarter

Patriots TD: Laurence Maroney 1 yd run (Stephen Gostkowski kick), 14:57. Drive: 12 plays, 56 yards in 5:04 Patriots 7-3

4th Quarter

Giants TD: David Tyree 5 yd pass from Eli Manning (Lawrence Tynes kick), 11:05. Drive: 6 plays, 80 yards in 3:47 Giants 10-7

Patriots TD: Randy Moss 6 yd pass from Tom Brady (Stephen Gostkowski kick), 2:42. Drive: 12 plays, 80 yards in 5:12 Patriots 14-10

Giants TD: Plaxico Burress 13 yd pass from Eli Manning (Lawrence Tynes kick), 0:35. Drive: 12 plays, 83 yards in 2:07 Giants 17-14

PLAYER STATS: GIANTS

PASSING	CP/AT	YDS	TD	INT
Manning	19/34	255	2	1

RUSHING	ATT	YDS	TD	LG
Bradshaw	9	45	0	13
Jacobs	14	42	0	7
Manning	3	4	0	5

RECEIVING	REC	YDS	TD	LG
Toomer	6	84	0	38
Smith	5	50	0	17
Tyree	3	43	1	32
Burress	2	27	1	14
Boss	1	45	0	45
Bradshaw	1	3	0	3
Hedgecock	1	3	0	3

PLAYER STATS: PATRIOTS

PASSING	CP/AT	YDS	TD	INT
Brady	29/48	266	1	0

RUSHING	ATT	YDS	TD	LG
Maroney	14	36	1	9
Faulk	1	7	0	7
Evans	1	2	0	2

RECEIVING	REC	YDS	TD	LG
Welker	11	103	0	19
Faulk	7	52	0	14
Moss	5	62	1	18
Stallworth	3	34	0	18
Maroney	2	12	0	8
Brady	1	3	0	3

TOTAL 2007-2008 PLAYER STATISTICS

REGULAR SEASON

PASSING

Player	G	GS	CMP	ATT	PCT	YDS	YDS/ATT	TD	INT	1ST	SCK	RTG
Manning, Eli	16	16	297	529	56.1	3336	6.3	23	20	165	27	73.9
Lorenzen, Jared	2	0	4	8	50.0	28	3.5	0	0	1	1	58.3
Wright, Anthony	2	0	1	7	14.3	12	1.7	0	0	1	0	39.6
Total:			302	544	55.5	3376	6.2	23	20	167	28	73.0

RUSHING

Player	G	GS	RUSH	YDS	AVG	LG	TD	1ST	STF	YDL	FUM	FBL
Jacobs, Brandon	11	9	202	1009	5.0	43	4	49	13	33	4	3
Ward, Derrick	8	5	125	602	4.8	44	3	28	8	13	2	1
Droughns, Reuben	16	2	85	275	3.2	45	6	27	12	23	1	0
Bradshaw, Ahmad	6	0	23	190	8.3	88	1	6	3	6	0	0
Manning, Eli	16	16	29	69	2.4	18	1	9	13	19	4	1
Shockey, Jeremy	14	14	1	6	6.0	6	0	0	0	0	0	0
Moss, Sinorice	12	2	1	4	4.0	4	0	0	0	0	0	0
Lorenzen, Jared	2	0	1	2	2.0	2	0	0	0	0	0	0
Wright, Anthony	2	0	1	-1	-1.0	-1	0	0	1	1	0	0
Hixon, Domenik	2	1	1	-8	-8.0	-8	0	0	1	8	0	0
Total:			469	2148	4.6	88	15	119	51	103	11	5

RECEIVING

Player	G	GS	REC	YDS	AVG	LG	TD	1ST	YAC	TRGT
Burress, Plaxico	16	16	70	1025	14.6	60	12	49	286	141
Toomer, Amani	16	15	59	760	12.9	40	3	42	201	104
Shockey, Jeremy	14	14	57	619	10.9	29	3	33	262	93
Moss, Sinorice	12	2	21	225	10.7	20	0	11	68	37
Ward, Derrick	8	5	26	179	6.9	17	1	7	189	40
Jacobs, Brandon	11	9	23	174	7.6	34	2	7	190	38
Boss, Kevin	7	2	9	118	13.1	23	2	8	30	14
Smith, Steve	5	0	8	63	7.9	12	0	4	21	14
Droughns, Reuben	16	2	7	49	7.0	11	0	1	44	15
Hedgecock, Madison	9	9	6	45	7.5	9	0	0	29	11
Mix, Anthony	1	0	3	39	13.0	21	0	2	19	5
Tyree, David	2	0	4	35	8.8	24	0	2	27	5
Matthews, Michael	10	6	6	28	4.7	6	0	0	16	13
Bradshaw, Ahmad	6	0	2	12	6.0	11	0	1	9	5
Hixon, Domenik	2	1	1	5	5.0	5	0	0	1	1
Total:			302	3376	11.2	60	23	167	1392	537

KICKING

Player	G	1-29	30-39	40-49	50+	FG-ATT	PCT	LG	XP-ATT	PTS
Tynes, Lawrence	16	10-11	5-8	8-8	0-0	23-27	0.9	48	40-42	109

DEFENSE

Player	G	GS	TK	AST	SCK	STF	FF	FR	PD	INT	INTYDS	DEFTD
Pierce, Antonio	16	16	76	26	1	6	1	2	8	1	28	0
Wilson, Gibril	13	13	70	14	0	3	0	1	7	4	12	0
Madison, Sam	16	15	60	8	1	3.5	1	1	14	4	59	0
Mitchell, Kawika	16	16	54	22	3.5	2.5	2	1	4	1	20	2
Tuck, Justin	16	2	46	17	10	8	2	0	1	0	0	0
Strahan, Michael	15	15	45	12	9	8	1	1	2	0	0	0
Butler, James	13	12	42	16	0	1.5	0	1	7	1	0	0
Umenyiora, Osi	14	16	41	11	13	3	5	2	0	0	0	1
Ross, Aaron	14	9	35	7	1.5	0.5	0	0	9	3	51	1
Kiwanuka, Mathias	10	9	33	11	4.5	3	0	0	4	0	0	0
Robbins, Fred	16	15	31	11	5.5	2	0	0	1	0	0	0
Cofield, Barry	14	15	29	5	1	2.5	0	0	1	0	0	0
Dockery, Kevin	11	6	29	11	0	1	1	1	8	0	0	0
Torbor, Reggie	11	6	21	10	1	1	0	0	1	0	0	0
Johnson, Michael	11	5	20	2	0	3	0	0	2	0	0	0
McQuarters, R.W.	10	2	13	1	0	0	0	1	1	0	0	0
Webster, Corey	10	3	13	1	0	0	0	0	3	1	34	1
Dahl, Craig	6	2	11	3	0	0	0	0	0	0	0	0
Blackburn, Chase	13	0	5	0	0	0	0	1	0	0	0	0
Wilkinson, Gerris	5	0	5	3	0	2	0	0	1	0	0	0
Davis, Russell	4	0	2	3	0	0	0	0	1	0	0	0
Tollefson, Dave	2	0	2	1	0	0.5	0	0	0	0	0	0
Wright, Manuel	2	0	2	0	0	0	0	0	0	0	0	0
Alford, Jay	1	0	1	0	1	0	0	0	0	0	0	0
Bradshaw, Ahmad	6	0	1	0	0	0	1	1	0	0	0	0
Total:			687	195	52	51	14	22	75	15	204	5

POST-SEASON

PASSING

Player	G	GS	CMP	ATT	PCT	YDS	YDS/ATT	TD	INT	1ST	SCK	RTG
Manning, Eli	4	4	72	119	60.5	854	7.2	6	1	46	9	95.7

RUSHING

Player	G	GS	RUSH	YDS	AVG	LG	TD	1ST	STF	YDL	FUM	FBL
Bradshaw, Ahmad	4	0	48	208	4.3	13	1	9	2	2	0	0
Jacobs, Brandon	4	4	62	197	3.2	12	3	10	4	7	1	0
Manning, Eli	4	4	8	10	1.3	5	0	2	2	2	1	0
Total:			118	415	3.5	13	4	21	8	11	3	0

RECEIVING

Player	G	GS	REC	YDS	AVG	LG	TD	1ST	YAC	TRGT
Toomer, Amani	4	4	21	280	13.3	52	3	15	90	26
Burress, Plaxico	4	4	18	221	12.3	32	1	13	49	30
Smith, Steve	4	0	14	152	10.9	22	0	9	36	26
Boss, Kevin	4	4	5	90	18.0	45	0	4	37	12
Tyree, David	3	0	4	47	11.8	32	1	2	3	8
Jacobs, Brandon	4	4	4	29	7.3	11	1	2	45	5
Bradshaw, Ahmad	4	0	4	27	6.8	9	0	1	27	6
Hedgecock, Madison	2	3	2	8	4.0	5	0	0	7	2
Total:			72	854	11.9	52	6	46	294	537

KICKING

Player	G	1-29	30-39	40-49	50+	FG-ATT	PCT	LG	XP-ATT	PTS
Tynes, Lawrence	4	2-2	2-3	1-2	0-0	5-7	0.7	35.6	10-10	25

DEFENSE

Player	G	GS	TK	AST	SCK	STF	FF	FR	PD	INT	INTYDS	DEFTD
Butler, James	4	4	22	5	0	1.5	0	0	1	0	0	0
Pierce, Antonio	4	4	21	3	0	0	0	0	1	0	0	0
Strahan, Michael	4	4	19	3	2	2	2	0	1	0	0	0
Wilson, Gibril	4	4	15	12	0	0	0	0	3	0	0	0
Mitchell, Kawika	4	3	12	8	2	0	0	0	1	0	0	0
Tuck, Justin	4	0	11	3	2	1.5	1	0	1	0	0	0
Ross, Aaron	4	3	9	3	0	0	0	0	1	0	0	0
Umenyiora, Osi	3	4	8	2	0	1.5	0	1	1	0	0	0
Torbor, Reggie	4	4	7	4	1	1.5	0	0	0	0	0	0
Webster, Corey	4	4	6	4	0	1	0	1	5	2	9	0
Dockery, Kevin	2	0	5	1	0	0	0	0	1	0	0	0
Robbins, Fred	3	4	5	2	0	0	0	0	0	0	0	0
Wilkinson, Gerris	2	1	5	2	0	0	0	0	0	0	0	0
McQuarters, R.W.	3	1	4	1	0	1	0	0	3	3	11	0
Johnson, Michael	4	0	3	0	0	0	0	0	2	0	0	0
Madison, Sam	2	0	3	1	0	0	0	0	1	0	0	0
Alford, Jay	2	0	2	2	1	0	0	0	0	0	0	0
Cofield, Barry	3	4	2	1	0	0	0	0	0	0	0	0
Pope, Geoffrey	2	0	1	0	0	0	0	0	0	0	0	0
Total:			160	58	8	10	3	4	22	5	20	0

TEAM TOTALS

REGULAR SEASON

	Giants	Opp.
First Downs	321	288
Third Downs Made/Att	91/219	73/211
Fourth Downs Made/Att	6/17	10/16
Avg. Time of Possession	31:21	28:38
Total Yardage	5302	4880
Yards/Game	331.4	305
Yards/Scoring Play	15.1	19.2
Penalties	77	118
Penalty Yards	652	874
Fumbles/Lost	26/14	24/10
Interceptions Thrown	20	15
Sacked	28	53
2-Point Conversions Made/Att	2/2	3/3
1st Quarter Scoring	58	82
2nd Quarter Scoring	128	100
3rd Quarter Scoring	73	72
4th Quarter Scoring	118	97
Overtime Scoring	0	0

POST-SEASON

	Giants	Opp.
First Downs	73	78
Third Downs Made/Att	23/53	27/54
Fourth Downs Made/Att	1/2	0/3
Avg. Time of Possession	31:52	28:46
Total Yardage	1222	1145
Yards/Game	305.5	286.3
Yards/Scoring Play	12.8	12.1
Penalties	18	27
Penalty Yards	155	181
Fumbles/Lost	7/1	6/2
Interceptions Thrown	1	5
Sacked	9	8
2-Point Conversions Made/Att	0/0	0/0
1st Quarter Scoring	13	7
2nd Quarter Scoring	24	31
3rd Quarter Scoring	17	10
4th Quarter Scoring	28	17
Overtime Scoring	3	0

Acknowledgments

One Giant Leap, a celebration of the Giants' season is the third book *The Star-Ledger* has published over the past 13 months. Previous books were *Rutgers, An Amazing Season* and *25, The History of the Devils in New Jersey.*

Once again, **Seth Siditsky,** *The Star-Ledger's* deputy director of photography for sports, and **Pim Van Hemmen,** the assistant managing editor for photography edited the book. They gathered the content, edited the photos, liaised with the publishing house and checked the many proofs.

A newspaper needs good beat writers to cover its local teams. **Mike Garafolo,** the Giants writer, is one of the best in the business. Only Mike could predict that Lawrence Tynes would kick a crucial 47 yard field goal … five months before it would actually happen.

Columnist **Steve Politi,** reporter **Kevin Manahan** and reporter **Brad Parks** also contributed their insightful words on the team.

Jerry Izenberg, one of only a handful of reporters to have covered every Super Bowl, provided the foreword for the book.

Sports editor **Tom Bergeron** spent countless hours, in the midst of Super Bowl mania, gathering the words for the book.

When deadlines are tight (two weeks from conception to final proofs) things can get hairy. We are fortunate that copy editors **Julie Cirelli-Heurich, Tracy Politowicz,** and **Mark DiMartini** and deputy sports editor **Matt Romanoski** were willing to jump into the fray at the last minute to assist with proofreading.

Dave Hawkins, deputy director of photography for production, and night photo editors **John Figlar** and **Mitch Seidel** stayed late into the night to pounce on errors and help gather all of the pictures.

Assistant sports photo editor **Steve Miller** and assistant photo editor **Natalia Jimenez** dug through the photo archives and outtakes to find hidden gems that we missed during the regular season.

Where would we be without **Brad Fenison** at Pediment Publishing? Only Brad would put up with newspaper editors who deliver the content two minutes before deadline. Only his patience supercedes his design abilities and fast delivery.

Bob Provost and **Doug Hutton** of *The Star-Ledger's* marketing department provided the impetus for the project.

Special thanks goes to photo assignment editor **Michelle Segall** for her tireless efforts in assigning the photographers and to **Sharon Russell** and **Tim Scrivani** for running digital camera cards at the Super Bowl.

Last, but not least, we need to acknowledge the photographers who braved the sidelines from Tampa Bay to Green Bay and everywhere in between. Without **Noah Addis, Jennifer Brown, Joe Epstein, Tim Farrell, Chris Faytok, Saed Hindash, Tony Kurdzuk, Scott Lituchy, Andrew Mills, John Munson, John O'Boyle,** and **William Perlman** there would not have been a book.